Research Quests of Young Intellectuals

Edited by
Kevin Jung

The Hermit Kingdom Press
Highland Park * Seoul * Bangalore * Cebu

Research Quests of Young Intellectuals
Copyright ©2011 The Hermit Kingdom Press

Paperback ISBN13: 978-1-59689-168-5

Write To Address:
The Hermit Kingdom Press
P. O. Box 1226
Highland Park, NJ 08904-1226
The United States of America

Library of Congress Cataloging-in-Publication Data

Research quests of young intellectuals / edited by Kevin Jung.
 p. cm.
Includes bibliographical references.
ISBN 978-1-59689-168-5 (pbk. : alk. paper)
I. Jung, Kevin.
AC5.R465 2011
081--dc23
                          2011043540

Dedicated to Old Tappan High School

Contents

Acknowledgement

I would like to thank first of all, my father, Kyung Min Jung, and my mother, Doctor Kyung Hee Kim, MD, for their constant support of me throughout my life. Without my father and my mother's support, this book would not have been possible. They have been constant, positive moral support in my life.

I would like to thank The Hermit Kingdom Press for believing in me and selecting me to be the editor of this important research book. I have published my autobiography in the book, *The Life Stories of Korean American Youth*, by Grace Jungmin Ko. I am thankful that they thought positively about my writing in that book, so that they entrusted me with this great responsibility to be the editor for this impressive book. Since they have faith in me that I will become great, I will not let them down as I'm resolved to succeed in my life as a leader of my generation.

I would also like to thank my marketing teacher at Old Tappan High School, in Old Tappan, New Jersey, Ms. Anita Parciasepe and Economics and history teacher, Mr. Edward Pasino, for being an encouragement to me. They have encouraged me to pursue my dream to become a millionaire entrepreneur who develops tourism in the Third World.

I would also like to thank my friends at Old Tappan High School who have been particularly supportive, Nick Lee, Jirou Lee, and Sonia Kim. Their friendship means a lot to me and their friendship gave me energy to edit this book, enthusiastically and effectively.

I would like to dedicate this book to Old Tappan High School because teachers, staff, and students at Old Tappan High School have inspired me in many different ways, and I know my achieving future greatness will due to in important part to their contribution in my life. Thank you Old Tappan High School!

Introduction

This book of research contains impressive array of research by young intellectuals who want to be future leaders of America and the world. Ariel Raimundo Choi writes a research essay about neuroscience based on three years of research at Regis High School and summer-long research at Hunter College. Ray wants to be a neuro-surgeon and a leading global medical researcher in the future. He is one of the brightest Koreans in the state of New Jersey and New York, so I have no doubt that he will achieve his goal. David Cho also submitted his research in the area of science (on cancer) and exhibits high potential for someone who is in the 9th grade. Perhaps, his sister, who is an alumna of Columbia University, had an impact on him and his research, because his sister hopes to become a globally significant medical doctor. Another research in the area of sciences was conducted by Nick Choi, a straight-A 9th grader from Demarest High School, the sister school of Old Tappan High School (they both make up the Northern Valley Regional High Schools in the Bergen County of the state of New Jersey) who wants to be a famous dental surgeon in the future. Nick researched dental diseases. I have no doubt that he will make a mark as a famous dentist in the future.

This book also contains serious study in non-science areas. William Mun has researched Edgar Allen Poe. William analyzed Poe's poems, such as "The Raven." William has used poetic devices to explain the power of Poe's poetry.

Furthermore, William has examined Poe's life and shows the connection between his life and his poetry. His twin brother, Andrew Mun, did research in the area of fine arts. Andrew Mun examines Giotto and the Italian Renaissance. Andrew examines elements of Giotto's frescoes and explains the background history of Giotto's art. The Mun brothers plan to create a billion-dollar computer software company in the future, and I have no doubt that they will succeed in their endeavor. I believe anyone who can effectively analyze Poe's poetry and Giotto's art that well can do anything in their life.

There is another art history contribution from a friend of mine at Old Tappan High School. Jongho Lee has written on the Hudson River School and the American art. Jongho wants to be a world famous artist and art historian. And knowing him well personally, I am positive that he will achieve his goal. James Park, Jr. writes on another area of history. James Park, Jr. discusses Byzantine history. In particular, James Park, Jr. examines the life and legacy of emperor Justinian. Furthermore, James Park, Jr. explains the struggles of western civilization at the time of Justinian in Rome, in Spain, and in Constantinople. A son of a famous Korean entrepreneur, James wants to be an entrepreneur himself. He wants to create a computer company in the future and become the next generation Steve Jobs. Reading his impressive research, I'm sure that he can achieve his goal.

I have myself contributed two research essays for this book. The first one is related to my primarily area of interest, Hotel and Hospitality Management. I want to be a successful entrepreneur who develops a successful tourism industry in the Third World. Therefore, I have examined the concept of branding, customer service, effective management, and various strategies for creating a multimillion-dollar tourism industry.

The second research essay is written in Korean. This research also is, in a way, related to tourism. In the Korean essay, I wrote about South Sudan's independence and the potential to develop South Sudan for tourism industry. This was a good case study for me since South Sudan is a Third World country. It helped me to affirm that developing tourism in the Third World is not only viable, but also profitable.

I am honored to be the editor of this book of research essays, because the contributions are significant and have much to teach everyone. Also, I know that all the writers will be very successful leaders in the future.

"How to Become the Best Hotel Entrepreneur?"

Kevin Jung

Best Education

How does Cornell University help to achieve as an entrepreneur? As a student planning to become a successful entrepreneur in the hospitality industry in the Third World, I understand the quality and value of Cornell's advanced education, which focuses on making leaders of the hospitality industry.

Cornell University's School of Hotel Administration's specific path to success, planned education and the faculty are, by far, the best in the world in the education of students to become leaders of the hospitality industry. I have read the most recent book produced by Cornell University School of Hotel Administration on hospitality and learned about the cutting edge faculties and the experienced training they provide as an educating institution. There are 70 faculty members, and 28 of them contributed in writing chapters for the book. The Cornell's School of Hotel Administration faculty had a combination of 450 years of teaching, 400 years of research, 250 years of hospitality industry experience and 360 years of consulting with the industry (p. 4, Starman, Corget and Verma). The education by the faculty of Cornell University's School of Hotel Administration is what I believe to be the best in producing the most successful entrepreneur in tourism and hospitality.

Cornell's School of Hotel Administration was founded in 1922 by request of hotel industry to promote educations for owners of hospitality and tourism industry, so it is the oldest of its kind in the world. With the passage of time, Cornell School of Hotel Administration has built helpful knowledge base and scholarship in Hotel Administration. Examples of such knowledge is shown in the book by the faculty of Cornell University School of Hotel Administration, which states that "any successful hospitality operation – be it a hotel or restaurant, chain or independent, low cost provider or luxury establishment – requires an effectively performing individual operation.' (p. 2, Starman, Corgel and Verma). Cornell School of Hotel Administration is capable of teaching how to create wealth and success in the industry.

Furthermore, Cornell School of Hotel Administration's mission is to promote hospitality leadership by teaching, researching, and industry collaboration, so it can effectively produce leaders of the hospitality and tourism industry. There are several crucial elements to achieving leadership in hospitality and tourism industry, and I will discuss them, here.

Brand

Brand is one of the best ways to increase benefit and profit. However, it is very important to choose between branding or independent operation, based on hospitality company's needs.

For some, independent operation can be better than branding. In parts of the world, such as areas in Europe and Asia, entrepreneurs can earn more profit possibility in an independent operation (p. 392, Kwortnik). STR global trend statistics shows that independent hotels earned much higher average daily rate (21.4%) and revenue per available room (17.5%) in 2010. These are results of certain regional or local markets.

However, Branding provides many other advantages. Brand is by definition uniqueness in name, logo, trade character, package design, or trade dress. These all contribute in distinguishing the product from their competitors. Also, it identifies 'you' apart from others to the costumer, protecting both parties from product imitators, by registering with a government agency responsible for overseeing property rights. The most important of all, brand promises uniform level of quality delivered by the brand. This enables consumers, who may not have ready access to complete information about their available choices, to make decisions benefiting the brand.

Furthermore, allying with an established brand brings number of advantages. It provides brand website, reservation system, marketing communication programs, service standards, training programs, sales and marketing teams, referral and royalty programs, also in booking meetings, incentive, conference, and exhibition of business. Despite the cost of brand affiliation, which is the second largest operation expense in most cases, franchisees usually support the cost for upgrades to the brand such as enhanced room amenities, bedding, and technology.

One of the most important in branding is to have 'promise'. It is the essence of both the value proposition to customers and the motivation for employees to live the brand. The promise must address wants and needs of the customer, convey experience that customers desire, and deliver, succinct, and compelling message. (p. 400, Kwortnik) For example, Las Vegas promised 'what happens here, stays here,' which conveys the freedom, encouragement and fun. Also, Royal Caribbean Cruise Line conveyed in their slogan, 'get out there', the excitement. Both of the example slogans clarify the meaning easily understandable and catchy.

What comes after promise is the touch point. Touch point seemingly proves the promise that a company makes. However, touch point is as important as promise, because touch point is what brings customers 'back in'. Examples of touch points can be anything; design, quality of service, meal, activities, attractions, even objects. For example, brand hotel, W Hotel promises WoW experiment (p.402, Kwortnik), which is enjoying fun, whatever and whenever the customers want. Touch points in it are the fun (singing waiters, and water slides), excitement (bright colored interiors and large casinos), and novelty, (the towel animals and theme restaurants.)

Brand promises, and touch points all comes to one purpose; getting customer in. McDonald's wouldn't be so popular without establishing countless stores over the world.

Las Vegas won't have as much visitors were it only casinos in the middle of the desert. W Hotel won't seem much better than other hotels if it didn't have the exciting design, activities, and novelty. Increase in fame and customer service is for the same purpose, increase of benefit and profit.

Goal

The case study of Four Seasons, a brand, contains many valuable insights. Isadore Sharp's biography on his goal and vision to succeed in the hospitality shows ways to achieve success with branding.

Isadore Sharp is a risk taker who wanted to create a group of best hotels in the world. Isadore took risk in countless places. First of all, he had put up his first hotel, called The Four Seasons in Netanya, located 25 miles from Tel Aviv, Israel (p. 89, Sharp). Then, he wanted to specialize in only 5 star rooms and services, in contrast to other hotel brands, such as Westin, Marriott and Cyharaton, which then had variety of 3, 4, and 5 stars hotels to their brand. To make these decisions, Isadore had strength that overrode doubt, confidence to press on with an idea that no one else thought of. And it worked.

The kind of personality that Isadore has is what made the brand, Four Seasons. He always wanted something special, something different than anyone else's. Even though there were many cases where he was laughed at, ignored, and put down, he just didn't give up his decision when he thought it was right. He often researched in McDonald's and his hotels to find keys to solutions. He came up with an idea of supreme quality.

He thought quality is one of the most important aspects in succeeding. He says, "We are going to win on quality. Quality is far and away chief factor in competitiveness". He also adds, "Quality doesn't necessarily mean luxury. It means giving customers what they expect, meeting customer's expectations every time." (p. 93, Sharp)

Lower Class Workers and Customer Service

As Four Season's business model emphasizes, an important issue for hospitality business is motivating lower level workers on the floor to serve the customers to the benefit of the company. Perhaps, the Nordstrom model of management and customer service provides a helpful direction for hospitality business.

Since Everett Elmer and Lloyd Nordstrom bought the business from John W, in the late 1920's, they had a motto for the company. "Put as much responsibility (or freedom) as possible into the hands of as many people as possible." (p.108, Spector and Mc Carthy)

Nordstrom believed that most important function in the business is the sales person. And to make them motivated, Nordstrom empowers its employee to take ownership. That is, Nordstrom gives its people on the sales floor the freedom to make entrepreneurial decisions and management backs them on those decisions. In order to do so, Nordstrom gives commission sales and bonuses. Giving by working harder, Nordstrom sales people were often able to build loyal customer following. For example, one retired top Nordstrom sales woman once described her business as "one step shopping." What she did was, once when a customer wanted a case of hangers, she ordered them from her distribution center. Then another customer wanted to buy some of their long plastic garment

6

bags. Even though she didn't make commission on it, she believed that it's part of the service that she provided, so she worked to provide what the customer wanted.

Interestingly, Nordstrom encouraged dynamic tension among its employees for better service, and supported them 100%. Nordstrom established the term pace setters for the top sales people, which made all the other sales people a 'goal' they can achieve. Pace setters are chosen from most sales from December 16th to next December 15th. Pacesetters are given a certificate of merit, outstanding in their honor, business card with the pacesetter designation and 33% discount credit on any merchandize. However, not only did Nordstrom make competitive environment, but it also backed sales people 100%. This is a very important point. Many examples are evident which proves Nordstrom's support, one of which is shown when an employee gave away $3000 worth of merchandise for customer's damaged shirts. Nordstrom published an annual report to shareholders, entitled *A Company of Entrepreneurs*. Nordstrom stated, "You have all the support and all the tools. It's up to you to see where you would like to go with it". (p.116, Spector and McCarthy)

Furthermore, Nordstrom believes in every employment. That is, Nordstrom has confidence in decisions that employers make. "Sales person can make the decisions even if it's wrong." Len Kuntz said, when one of his sales people asked him for an advice on how to accommodate a customer's request. From the confidence, comes employer's small gestures. The small gestures which Robert Spector experienced in Starbucks made him have positive feelings towards Starbucks. When Robert brought a worn out bag to Starbucks to save 10 cents, an employer gave him a new bag for free. Even though it's monetary value is only 10 cents, the small gesture proved that it can turn people around.

Nordstrom also trusts in their employees on their return policy. When a customer is not satisfied with their purchase, for what ever reason, the store takes it back, no questions asked. For the frauds, Nordstrom decided not to punish the many for the few.

In order to build the trust and learn the system, all managers and buyers start up as salesman, because salesman gets to know what customers need and want. As for Nordstrom's system, the hospitality industry can absorb its tradition for the better environment for lower level workers.

Hiring New, Talented Workers

In business in general, hiring new workers is as important as training, branding and customer services mentioned before. That is because "A single bad recruit can poison the mood of an otherwise effective team." (p. 88, Inghiller and Solomon)

Before hiring any workers, Leonardo Inghilleri and Micah Solomon advise to have five traits covered in the book *Exceptional Service Exceptional Profit*. The five traits mentioned in the book go together in hiring employees with good personality. First, an employer must have genuine personal warmth, or to have kindness. That is because, customers, like many people everywhere, are superb at detecting counterfeit warmth. Then, empathic skill is required. An employer with warmth and empathic skill, unlike employer without empathic skill, has ability to understand what another human being is going through and knows how to interact helpfully in any situation. Third, an optimistic upbeat attitude is valued. This trait is especially important because service can be draining, but keeping the positive attitude in business is directly connected with success and failure. Fourth, trait that an employer must have is team orientation. Team orientation is very important because the team's working phase is dependant on the slowest working employee. Attitude, such as "you know I can handle it all myself," will never be helpful for the business. Last but not least, is conscientiousness, which is a broad trait that subsumes concepts like responsibility, work ethic, diligence, and attention in getting details right. Having all four traits but not having conscientiousness can horribly mess up the business.

Moreover, Leonardo and Micah emphasize in making the perfect day one for the employees. Day one in any business, organization or any other group is one of the most important days, because it only comes once. Also, the first impression that an employee makes on the first day is crucial for the entire working experience for the employee. On the first day, employees are disoriented, and during the period of disorientation, people are particularly susceptible to adopting new rules, goals, and values. (p. 91, Inghiller and Solomon) It is important to install most useful, positive attitudes, beliefs, and goals, not mere practical know-how's. It is important to make the new employee understand the goal of creating the best experience with the business for the customer. In order to achieve the understanding, the company must show their attitudes towards that employee in following ways: clean, perfectly orientated room, perfect visuals, simple refreshments, and use of only good quality, edited, up to date handouts.

All the following, the five traits and first impression is crucial, because hiring new employee is critical for every

9

business. Every business must choose an employee who has 'talent,' rather than who has specific skills for specific jobs. The employee must be a friendly, insightful, and responsible applicant, who can make people feel comfortable. For this reason, it is effective to hire employees who have settled five traits with empathy, energetic, and cognitive flexibility.

Solving Mistakes

Every business makes mistakes, but what's important is how the business responds to that mistake. Denny Meyer in the 'Setting the Table' tells us how to approach the mistake, and make it into chance.

"The road to success is paved with mistakes well handled'" (p. 220, Meyer), said Stanley Marcus, whose family founded the luxury department store Neiman Marcus in Dallas, 1907. As the author, Danny repeated it over and over, thinking about the statement. Then he realized that perfection is impossible in business, and as Irving Harris said, "The definition of business is problems." The success lies not in the elimination of problems, but in the art of creative profitable problem solving. He further explains that the best companies are those that distinguish themselves by solving problems most effectively. As Denny visualizes, we must expect the unexpected in looking at the waves while surfing. Employers must know how to ride the waves that are unexpected.

In solving mistakes, we must know how to solve mistakes. First, employers must be aware of making mistakes. Second, employees must acknowledge themselves along with customers, telling them what happened. Third, Employees must apologize; making ridiculous excuses won't get the customer anywhere. Fourth, the action; action must be made at that instant or at least 24 hours. Last step is to show additional generosity. Few kindness of giving additional wine or so makes the mistake turn around into chance. Also, while knowing how to solve mistakes, employees can add few bits of humor, if the mistakes are not big.

To solve mistakes, the most important aspect is to end in the 'great last chapter' of "Mistakes that happen happened" (p222, Meyer). There are no going back to fix mistakes. However, business can turn the mistake around into chance by using the controllable part of that mistake, the last respond. Customers will tell people around them about the mistakes, but if business adds a good last response, the image turns green for the business. For example, if a customer spills a cup of wine, although the customer had made the mistake, pouring another cup of wine makes the customer tell people around him or her about the free refill he or she had. In the same way, when customers who come into a restaurant with 5 others order a meal, and on the way to the table, waiter drops one dish, by giving an additional soup or a salad to the left out customer along with remade meal turns on the green light.

Marketing and Pricing

What makes up the actual revenue in business is the marketing and pricing. These two factors are especially critical in the hotel industry since little change can lead to millions of dollars in profit of loss.

Since the World War 2, marketing and advertising became increasingly important. That is because many people now have extra money and cheaper transportation fee to move around for a period. That said, branding, as I have discussed earlier became one of the key factors of the hotel industry, because of character and expectation of the service which every individual can expect from hotels of the brand. At the same time, it enables broader reaches of advertising and sales. Since the technological development, thanks to the internet, the face of marketing has changed and is still growing in increasing rate. Websites, with user-friendly ways for an individual customer to make and pay for a reservation easier now have become ever-growing section of the market.

Pricing is the most important factor to handle in focused, quietly, and concentrated manner. Not only does it make major changes in revenue, but also, it also shows the reputation. For a short term, sales discounts will probably increase the sale for that season. For example, Rolls Royce can sell cars at 50% discount during bad seasons, and earn as much profit as the good season. However, for the long term, the brand could lose its reputation of being one of the most expensive, luxurious cars.

Pricing policies are primarily important in the business's revenue. First of all, "Understanding and mastering this relationship between price and volume is one of the key skills of hotel management" (p. 89, Venison). Price verses occupancy and operating cost behind occupancy must be taken seriously to determine their rate. Also, for a hotel industry, who's operating in more complex markets needs menu of prices called rack rate. Rack rate is the cost of each room in each season for individuals who do not seek discounts. Because of the seasons and events in a local community, rack rate should vary accordingly to seasons or weekly demands. A bad example of not considering rack rate was when one Chinese hotel charged same price for all rooms for the whole year around. Because of it, many tour operators marked up prices for their benefits during the good seasons, and this was bad for business. When the "problem" was fixed and pricing adjusted according to seasons, the revenue increased by a million dollars. One last thing to consider in pricing, particularly in the Third World market, is the currency. One traveling from U.S. will observe different price than one in, say, China. Because of the inflation and currency, wholesalers can charge at a cheaper price than to a foreign customer which the customer, at the end will end up paying higher price than what was promised.

World Wide Web

Utilizing modern marketing tools such as World Wide Web is as important as pricing. Perhaps, it could be more important in a way, since it brings the customers into the actual hotel.

Many people in the world now use the internet. Along with other forms of advertising, websites have become one of the key advertisers around the world. However, how fantastic the website or the hotel is doesn't matter unless the business drives customer into the website and convert them into potential customers (p. 147, Cooper and Whittington) PPC (Pay per click) offered by many search engines, is one of the most effective tools in advertising. Not only does it pop up when the target audience search for the phrase, but it also is easier to compare, control, and measure. PPC can also provide researchable information which is available from recording information through the links which customer came from. Also, it shows what phrase motivated the customers into the websites. Because of this, it is easier to control the phrases, on and off dates, and budget. With the records, it is easier to measure the result and improve on it.

To drive the customers into the websites, it is smart to use a joint venture, working with another business which is targeting the same audience (p. 151, Cooper and Whittington). Or the businesses can piggy back on the travel and entertainment websites on the events, such as a concert in the local area. However, the ads must be unique with striking headlines and features so that it is 'my business that the customers click for, not the others'. There are many other ways to build traffic, such as writing a post, article, linking from printed materials, and blogging. Blogging could be one of the most effective ways, in website advertising, because it updates day by day or even hour by hour. Blogs also can build a stronger relationship with the target audiences, and post events and news around the area without annoying the audience.

Identifying target group for marketing comes before launching the advertisements. In this regard, Professor Michael Lynn at Cornell School of Hotel Administration is helpful in the new Cornell faculty book, in chapter 23, in addressing the issue.

Segmenting

Marketing strategies, widely known as STP, has three steps: to segment, target, and position. This approach suggests that the mass market consists of some number of relatively homogeneous groups, each with distinct needs and desires. However, segmenting disregards large portion of the market. For example, Nielsen Claritas's segmentation shows how it only includes a small segment of the whole population. "Money and brain segment includes high incomes, advanced degrees, and sophisticated tastes to match their credentials. Many of which are city dwellers, predominantly white population with a high concentration of Asian Americans, are married couples with few children who live in fashionable homes on small, manicured lots." (p. 354, Lynn)

However, how many segments the business focuses on depends on the answer depended on the business, the market, and customers. Because of this reason, conducting own study on marketing research is the best way for a business. Not only because it's the business's own records, but also because business can freely group the segment that contain customer who are similar to another, distinct group that is, large enough and reachable by media and stable.

Conclusion

I have looked at many important aspects of making the best hotel: branding, making a goal, providing great customer service, hiring competitive workers, solving mistakes, online marketing, pricing, and segmenting. All these aspects can tegether maximize benefit and profit when a great manager connects each of them.

Works Cited

Cooper, Caroline, and Lucy Whittington. Hotel Success Handbook: Practical Sales and Marketing Actions, Ideas and Tips to Get Results for Your Small Hotel, B&B, or Guest Acommodation. London: MX Pub., 2010. Print.

Inghilleri, Leonardo, and Micah Solomon. Exceptional Service, Exceptional Profit: the Secrets of Building a Five-star Customer Service Organization. New York: American Management Association, 2010. Print.

Meyer, Danny. Setting the Table: the Transforming Power of Hospitality in Business. New York: HarperCollinsPublishers, 2006. Print.

Sharp, Isadore. "Chapter 9." Four Seasons: the Story of a Business Philosophy. New York, NY: Portfolio, 2009. Print.

Spector, Robert, and Patrick D. McCarthy. The Nordstrom Way to Customer Service Excellence: a Handbook for Implementing Great Service in Your Organization. Hoboken, NJ: John Wiley & Sons, 2005. Print.

Sturman, Michael C., Jack B. Corgel, and Rohit Verma. The Cornell School of Hotel Administration on Hospitality: Cutting Edge Thinking and Practice. Hoboken, NJ: Wiley, 2011. Print.

Venison, Peter. 100 Tips for Hoteliers: What Every Successful Hotel Professional Needs to Know and Do. New York: IUniverse, 2005. Print.

"The Significance of the Hudson River School"
Jongho Lee

Many artists among the early years of America were portrait painters for famous politicians. However, the painters in the Hudson River School were the first ones to paint landscape paintings in America.[1] What made this group of talented artists different from the landscape painters in Europe were their beliefs behind their artworks and the different use of colors. It is important to understand their beliefs and background to comprehend the significance they had. The

---

[1] Thomas Hampson, "Hudson River School." PBS: Public Broadcasting Service. Public Broadcasting Service. Web. 30 June 2011. <http://www.pbs.org/wnet/ihas/icon/hudson.html#topofpage>.

Hudson River School left an impact on America, showed unique ideas different than any European painter had.

The Hudson River School and their style of art was popular starting in 1820 and started to fade out in about 1870 to 1880.[2] The landscapes painted by the artists of the Hudson River School are primarily characterized by the realistic, detailed portrayal of nature. This was when a different style of art other than the European, was first painted in America. The name came from the first group of artists, who usually stayed near New York for inspiration for their paintings. Even though many artists including Thomas Cole, who is recognized as the founder of the Hudson River School studied in Europe at first, they wanted to set a unique style of painting that would symbolize America.[3] The name most familiarized with the Hudson River School is Thomas Cole. He is known primarily to be the founder of the Hudson River School, and the mentors of many second generation painters.[4] Thomas Cole was a man of many talents, and a "...unusual combination of writer, poet, philosopher, observer, and painter..."[5].

Thomas Cole was often called the father of the Hudson River School, due to tremendous effect on the beginning of this new group. To understand what kind of role he played in establishing this group, a brief look at his biography is necessary. Thomas Cole was born in Bolton, Lancashire, England in 1801. In 1818, he moved with his family to Ohio, where he started to learn how to paint portraits. Unfortunately, painting portraits proved to be a failure, and his interest started to move towards

---

[2] Wikipedia
[3] http://en.wikipedia.org/wiki/Thomas_Cole

[4] Matthew Baigell, *Thomas Cole*, (Watson-Guptill Publications),1988 pg 10
[5] Howatt, *The Hudson River and Its Painters*, pg 35

landscape painting as he moved to Pittsburg. Here, he studied with the members of the Pennsylvania Academy of the Fine Arts, and moved to New York with his mother and sister in 1825. When he moved to New York, an event that would be vital to the formation of the Hudson River School occurred. George W. Bruen bought three of his paintings, and also financed a trip to the Catskill Mountain House where Cole discovered and painted the beauty of the wilderness.[6] As he returned to New York, he gained the attention of Trumbull, who would contract him with many wealthy friends including Robert Gilmore and Daniel Warsworth, who later became important patrons of Thomas Cole. He also caught the attention of Durand, who would become a peer later on.[7]

Nationalism was one of the main overlaying themes in the paintings of the Hudson River School.[8] The American Revolution, and especially The War of 1812 sparked a great sense of nationalism for the citizens of the United States of America, and gave reason to be proud of their heritage. It showed Americans that even though they did not have a long history like Europe, they had something that even Europe did not possess. America was filled with nature and pastoral scenes, which was difficult to find in Europe. This became a basis for the Hudson River School's paintings; the nature represented the pride Americans had for their country.[9] In addition to nationalism, Romanticism was a strong base for many of these landscapes. Romanticism was an era where Europeans wanted to bring back the significance of nature in the midst of the

---

[6] http://www.thomascole.org/biography-of-thomas-cole/
[7] http://en.wikipedia.org/wiki/Thomas_Cole
[8] Howat, *The Hudson River and Its Painters*, pg 67
[9] *The Hudson River School: Nationalism, Romanticism, and the Celebration of the American Landscape*, pg 1.

Industrial Revolution. It revived some of the elements of medieval paintings, and focused on nature and its importance. Romanticism mixed with nationalism provided a strong theme for the painters, and are clearly recognizable in the paintings.[10]

.   Another important theme in the paintings was exploration. This was also what made the paintings different from European landscapes. The painters from the Hudson River School looked for environments to capture in their paintings, where European painters worked in their studios.[11] Exploration in this case can be taken two different ways: exploration as in exploring the unknown regions to capture in their landscape, and exploration with different techniques in painting to capture different styles and effects created when painting a landscape.[12] Artists such as Durand paints lights so differently that even most painters in the Hudson River School could not imitate his style of painting.[13]

The last theme that appears in many of the landscape painting is religion. Religion does not appear directly out of these beautiful landscapes, leading one to go in depth into the paintings to analyze them. For example, the painting Cathedral Forest by Alfred Bierstadt shows a landscape of massive trees and in the middle is two humans on horses, barely visible in the woods covered with giant trees. This is a perfect example where the Hudson River painters demonstrate the insignificance of human beings compared to the god given gifts such as nature. The Hudson River School thought that nature was one of god's greatest gifts, and in order to truly worship it, humans must

---

[10] Wikipedia
[11] Wikipedia
[12] Wikipedia
[13] *The Hudson River School: Nationalism,* part 1

coexist with nature and not try to overpower it. This belief of nature and god is what bonded many of the painters together.[14]

The finest works in the Hudson River School were done by Second Generation Painters. Many of the Second Generation painters were Thomas Cole's students, and they set an American style of painting which became known as Luminism.[15] Luminism was an important technique for the Hudson River School, because it was an effect used by many artists when painting water and sky. It is often used to depict calmness in a scene. [16] The difference between the primary Hudson River School painters and the secondary was that many famous second generation painters such as Church and Bierstadt were influenced by the Düsseldorf school of painting. The Düsseldorf school of painting is a group of painters that were taught at Düsseldorf academy in 1830 through 1840.[17] This familiarized them with even more different techniques of painting, making their artwork more stunning and realistic. For example, people lined up for hours just to see the exhibited work of Frederic Edwin Church's *Niagara*. In addition, many painters such as Gifford and Church were among the founders of the Metropolitan Museum of Art, which remains one of the biggest museums of America and even in the world.[18]

The Hudson River Painters were an amazing group of painters that were the first to leave an artistic imprint on the land of America. Starting with artists such as Thomas Cole, and then to artists like Church, the landscapes started fading away when people's attentions were diverted to manifesting the land,

---

[14] Wikipedia
[15] Wikipedia, luminism
[16] Wikipedia
[17] Wikipedia Dusseldorf school
[18] Hampson, Hudson River School, pg 15

and not coexisting with it. The overlaying themes of the landscapes will never be forgotten, and the landscapes would forever mark the unique painting styles that America developed.

"Lung Cancer"
David Cho

Lung cancer is one of the most common cancers in the world. It is a nightmare that creeps around the world. Despite all the negative effects of lung cancer, it also has positive effects such as making new discoveries in science and also building the knowledge of people in the world. Lung cancer is formed when the cells of the lungs grow in an uncontrolled way, creating a lump or what is known as a tumor, and can be either cancerous or not cancerous. Although many people believe that smoking is one of the only way of getting lung cancer, but also breathing in radon gas, and not having healthy diets can also lead to lung cancer. All of these are tied to several common sources like peer pressure, teen diets, and role models. Preventions are available in many different methods, with the help of government and professional study; lung cancer can be treated, and controlled.

Cigarettes are full of poison and toxic chemicals, the ingredients affect everything from the functioning of organ's to the body's immune system. The damages can be widespread and fatal. Nicotine is a very toxic chemical present in cigarettes; it can reach the brain in ten seconds. While taking a long drag of smoke, and enjoying the pleasure of tobacco smoking, the chemicals are slowly rotting the lungs and straining the body. Smoking causes around one in five deaths from heart disease, in younger people, three out of four deaths from heart disease are due to smoking. Data shows the rate of young smokers increased drastically since 1930s. Among the young smokers, many are teenagers, during the recent years, the age of teen smokers are decreasing, but more and more students come in contact with cigarettes and other drugs. There are many different factors that contribute to the rising number of young smokers; the influence could've come both from school and from home. Peer pressure is associated with smoking, many students were forced into smoking by their peers; they surrender and give in to smoking because they wanted to feel cool, and most importantly to fit in. Teenagers would really commit to be able to gain acceptance, no matter what the "entering fee" is, they would pay for it. Hollywood and other media productions associate smoking with manliness, and maturity; it would be natural for students at a young age to get influenced and brain washed into imitating smokers. At home, if the adolescent's parents or one family member smokes, that person has a higher chance of following his/her family "legacy" and pick up the habit. This also increases the chance of other household members getting smoking related. "Non-smokers living with smokers have for about a 25 percent increase in risk of death from heart attacks [and strokes]. One recent study in the British Medical Journal found that exposure to second hand smoke increases the risk of heart disease among non-smokers by as much as 60 percent. Adults should smoke as least as possible in front of teenagers, because they are at an age when the curiosity level is the highest. The term "curiosity killed the cat" can be applied to teenagers and smoking. If teenagers grow curious about smoking and try it they might soon be addicted to it and eventually die.

Radon gas is a colorless, and odorless that is radioactive gas which is created naturally in stones and soil. Breathing in excessive amount of radon over a long period of time can increase the chance of getting lung cancer. Fortunately, this problem can be eliminated by modern technology, and regular testing can ensure the safety of home owners. The government also provided help for the public. This is a very responsible and helpful way to protect the health of the public. There are websites and news articles published by government to inform the people about the importance of radon gas testing and the danger of radon gas. The Nova Scotia government took the role of advertising useful information by publishing an article with professional health officer's notice and research. The government has also done many things to alert the public about the dangerous and fatal results of smoking, effects of smoking was put into the health curriculum to educate the students who are curious about smoking. This definitely stopped many students from touching cigarettes. There are many health commercials shown on TV to inform the public the harmfulness of smoking, it has also prevented many attempted smokers from actually buying a pack of cigarette. The effects and illness associated with smoking usually cover the cigarette packages;

this is a big step for the government to take to help the public realize the harm of cigarettes. Other topics related to radon gas are air pollution and coal mining industries. Pollutants in air can create build-ups inside the lung, and contribute to lung cancer; it has been estimated that 5 to 7% of lung cancer in non smokers are due to outdoor air pollutions. Air pollution in Canada is already at the bottom of the list when compared with countries like China and India. Jobs like coal mining are very dangerous and can damage the lungs, because workers would stay underground for hours without fresh air, and also inhaling coal particles floating in the air. This type of long term occupational exposure may increase lung cancer risk up to 47%, (that is the average risk of lung cancer plus half again). Self-protection would be extremely important for those jobs; masks must be worn at all times. Basic knowledge of all the issues mentioned above and self-protection skills should eliminate those causes leading to lung cancer.

These days' people believe that being skinny and looks are everything, however, some go overboard. Those who starve or go on extreme diets are more likely to have lung cancer. "An unbalanced diet can cause problems with maintenance of body tissues, growth and development, brain and nervous system function, as well as problems with bone and muscle systems" (MyDietExercise.com, Unbalanced Diet). Girls especially, tend to have an idea that being skinny would make them look beautiful just like the models on TV (IBID). Unfortunately soon reports said that cancerous tumors were able to be found in people with an unbalanced diet. "It is one reason why 40 percent of cancer patients die from malnutrition or cachexia." (The Alternative Medicine Research Foundation, Sugar and Cancer). It is better to maintain a healthy diet instead of "dying" to be beautiful.

Lung cancer may sound like a terrifying disease that took over many lives, but it is not ineradicable, 15% of the patients will survive; it is a small percentage, but there is hope. The chance of survival will increase if the patient stays optimistic and the courage to fight for his/her life. There are different treatments that can be applied. Surgeries can remove tumors, radiation therapy kills cancer cells that cannot be removed by surgery; chemotherapy is killing cancer cells by taking drugs. The technology is already advanced enough to reduce or stop the growth of lung cancer. The public need to raise their caution towards smoking, air pollution, radon gas, unhealthy diets and many more other problems may contribute to lung cancer. Diseases is not scary, knowledge can help defend the health and battle with the illness. Nevertheless, "one ounce of cure is better than one liter of cure," is always better.

"Edgar Allen Poe: His Life and Poetry"
William Mun

Edgar Allen Poe was a very famous poet, author, critic and editor. He was also a part of the American Romantic Movement. Edgar Allen Poe was considered the creator of mystery fiction. Edgar was born in Boston, Massachusetts, and was orphaned when he was very young. Poe had ancestors who were agriculturists and artisans on one side, and actors on the other. The paternal side of the family had some claim to military distinction. Edgar's great-great grandfather, David Poe was a Protestant tenant farmer, in Cavan, Ireland. John, his son, married the daughter of an admiral and emigrated around 1750 to Lancaster County in Pennsylvania. John's eldest son had moved to America with them when he was only seven. He was named after his grandfather. David later moved to Baltimore in 1775, and earned a living there making spinning wheels. He later owned a dry goods store.

David Poe, a member of Captain John McClellan's Company of Baltimore troops in 1778-1779, was appointed Assistant Deputy Quartermaster and purchased supplies for the American Army. When General Lafayette returned to tumultuous acclaim in Baltimore in 1824, he inquired about his old friend David and paid tribute to his generosity during the war. Lafayette visited David Poe's grave. Poe had spent over $40,000 of his own money for the Revolutionary war, and was given the courtesy title and was always known as "General" Poe.

Edgar's maternal grandparents married in London in May, 1789. Henry Arnold was a mysterious figure, but Elizabeth, his wife, first appeared on stage at the Theatre Royal, Covent Garden in February, 1791. She made her last appearance in London on June, 1795. Elizabeth became a widow and along with her daughter, Eliza (Poe's mother), they moved to America. They arrived in January 1796. There, Elizabeth married her second husband, Charles Tubbs. He was an actor, singer, and pianist. Unfortunately, she disappeared from theatrical records in 1798 and died shortly after.

Eliza Arnold made her first debut in Boston. She was in theatre at age nine, a couple of months after her arrival from England. She became a rising star. In November 1796, the Portland Eastern Herald praised Eliza on her excellent performance in David Garrick's farce, *Miss in Her Teens*. They said she was exceeded all praises and even if she was very young, her powers as an actress "will do credit to any of her sex of maturer age." (Meyers, page 2)

Eliza, with her mother already dead, married Charles Hopkins in 1802, when she was just fifteen. Charles was an actor, just like her. Eliza also played as many as three hundred parts. These include Shakespeare's Juliet, Ophelia and Cordelia, and more.

Poe's father, David Poe Jr. who was three years older than Eliza, was born in Baltimore, in 1784. Though he was destined for law, he chose to leave it behind and join the Thespian Club in Baltimore, a place where young men learned how to read and perform plays. During his business trip to Norfolk, Virginia, he watched Eliza perform and fell in love with her in an instant. In 1806, after Eliza's first husband died, she married David Poe Jr. in Richmond. "The nineteen year old widowed actress had been in an extremely vulnerable position, and may have married David Poe (and perhaps Charles Hopkins) for protection as much as for love." (Meyers, p.3)

David was rather attractive and a person suitable for juvenile parts and romantic heroes. In his entire career, he has done 137 different roles, and a few were Shakespearean. But, unfortunately, many critics belittled him, saying that Eliza was much better than him. One critic stated that, "the gentleman was literally nothing." Eliza was extolled while David was harshly criticized in a written review few years later. One said, "a more wretched Alonzo have we never witnessed. This man was never destined for the high walks of the drama- a footman is the extent of what he ought to attempt... His person, voice, and non expression of countenance, all combine to stamp him- poh!" (Meyers, p. 3)

David Poe had a large temper, and was a heavy drinker. He found it hard to swallow all the insults that were thrown at him. He was enraged when the critic used his name as a pun.

At the beginning of the nineteenth century, most cities in America were too small to support a permanent theater company, and were forced to move from place to place. Eliza later died of a sickness, and David Poe abandoned the family. He was never seen again. There were rumors that he lived in a small cottage, and died shortly after Eliza's death. Rosalie and Edgar were separated. Edgar was sent to live with John and Frances Allen, but he was unofficially adopted. There, the Allens changed his name to Edgar Allen Poe.

John Allen was also an orphan and was born in 1779 in Glasgow. He immigrated to Richmond, Virginia, on January 195 and became a partner of Charles Ellis in November 1800. Their store, Ellis & Allen, exported many supplies. Later however, the store was changed to Allen & Ellis.

Allen was described as shrewd and good looking. He had dark curly hair, high forehead, small widely spaced eyes, Roman nose, sensual mouth and firm chin. But he was quick tempered. He later married Frances Valentine, who was eighteen. She fostered Edgar and nourished him. Edgar was baptized in 1812 and confirmed in 1825 as an Episcopalian. The Allens dressed him as a young prince, and took him to many exquisite resorts. But unlike Frances, John was much the opposite. He scolded Poe many times. Later, Poe went to the University of Virginia. Edgar had fallen in love with Sarah Royster before he went to the University of Virginia. But, tragedy struck and Poe wasted all of his money gambling and drinking alcohol. John was furious and displeased at what Edgar did. So, he refused to continue supporting Edgar. Therefore, the debt was big and Poe dropped out of college.

He then joined the military and lied about his age. Edgar started out as a private. He only received five dollars a month. He later became an artificer, and earned double the money. He eventually reached the highest level for non-commissioned officers. Edgar tried to leave the army early. John didn't seem to help at first, and later resented Poe, and Poe was discharged from the army. Edgar Allen Poe then decided to join West Point. John, on the other hand, married his second wife, Louisa Patterson, around that time.

After a while in West Point, Edgar decided he had enough and tried to leave. He purposefully got court marshaled, and was found guilty.

Jobs were very scarce for Poe, especially since he was poor, and lost connection with John. He married Virginia Clemm, who was thirteen and who was his cousin. Edgar tried to become a writer and met John P. Kennedy, a Baltimorean. Later, John introduced Edgar to Thomas White, editor of *Southern Literary Messenger*. Edgar became the assistant editor, but was fired after White caught him drinking. Edgar promised good behavior and White let him into the company again. Then, he became the assistant editor of *Burton's Gentlemen Magazine*. He made lots of articles, stories and reviews. After this, Poe announced that he would be starting his own journal *The Stylus*, but it was not published until after his death.

Edgar Poe then decided to join the Tyler Administrations. He hoped to be appointed in the Custom House with help from Robert, President Tyler's son. But he failed to show up to the meeting and missed his opportunity.

In the last few years, his wife, Virginia started to become ill and had tuberculosis. Poe started to drink even more because he was stressed. Later, he also became the editor of *Broadway Journal* and sole owner. His poem "The Raven" was a popular sensation, but he only received nine dollars. Edgar's *Broadway Journal* failed and he moved back to New York. His wife Virginia died, and Edgar tried to marry Sarah Whitman, but her mother broke them apart.

Edgar was found delirious on 1849. Joseph W. Walker found him in the streets and took him to the hospital. He died five days later. His death was unknown. But Edgar Allen Poe is still remembered today as a historical figure, and one to be commemorated.

Poems

Now, I will provide my own analysis of Edgar Allen Poe's poems:

Edgar had many poems, but one of the most mysterious was "Annabel Lee." It is about a person whom Edgar loved, and her name was Annabel Lee. The poem has many metaphors. The poem begins saying that Annabel was born in the kingdom by the sea. It is a metaphor saying that Annabel was born in a rich family. Their love for each other creates problems as the poem progresses. In the poem, it says, "the clouds surrounded her" which is another metaphor. The clouds are the people or comments that are trying to stop the love, because it is strange or jealous. And highborn kinsmen who take her away are actually rich upper-classmen. She is put in a sepulcher, another metaphor for her house, in which she is locked up. The "sea" emphasizes how far apart they are from each other. And then, she is killed. It means that she is not actually killed, but Edgar is heartbroken and he feels as though she is dead.

So, he is reminded of her every night, and he says, "And the stars never rise, but I see the bright eyes of Annabel Lee." It shows he will never forget her. And it is sad because she is forever locked up in the tomb, and never met Edgar again.

Edgar Allen Poe's poem, "The Conqueror Worm," gives many insights on Poe's life. This poem is described from the book of Genesis in the Bible. The story is about how Adam and Eve fell to their death.

"Lo!' tis a gala night, within the lonesome latter years," in the first two lines tells the setting of this poem. It is in a banquet at night, in the lonely years. In line three, it says, "angel throngs, bewinged, bedight." In the poem, there are a group of angels, with wings, shining brightly. "In veils and drowned in tears," in line four is describing the angels. The angels are crying, hiding in veils. The poem progresses, and comes to the important part. Line eight, the poem is saying music of the spheres. Spheres are circular shapes, and it symbolizes different worlds.

The next stanza begins with the words, "Mimes in the form of God on high." Metaphorically, it is saying that these people are "miming" or copying God. Then, it says, "Mutter and mumble low, and hither and thither fly- mere puppets thy who come and go." Poe is describing the angels in this scene. They are muttering, talking quietly, and flying back and forth like puppets, as Edgar says in this poem. "At bidding of vast formless things" in line thirteen is referring back to the spiritual angels, who are amorphous things. Then, after the poem says the scenery shifts to and fro, and things are unfolding suddenly.

"Flapping from out their condor wings, invisible woe!" So lines fifteen and sixteen are showing an invisible tragedy, that no one is aware of. "That motley drama- oh, be sure- it shall not be forgot!" This scene and drama won't be forgotten. As the poem comes to the climactic scene, the next line says, "with its phantom chased for evermore, by a crowd that seize it not." Edgar Allen Poe is creative with his word positioning, and he is saying this ghost will be pursued forever, by a crowd that can never grasp it. This phantom is evasive. "Through a circle that ever returneth in to the self- same spot." This sentence in line twenty and twenty one has Poe's word play again. It is a metaphor stating that the crowd will go a circle, and come back to the same spot again. And in line twenty two, it says, "And much of madness and more of sin." There is much craziness and people are doing horrible things.

"But see; amid the mimic rout." This means there are imitating victories. In the next line, it says, "A crawling shape intrudes!" In line twenty four this mysterious creature lurks, it is an illusion. Lines twenty five and twenty six say "A blood red thing that writhes from out, the scenic solitude." This blood red thing is actually a snake, in the book of Genesis. The snake is alone. "Angels sob at the vermin fangs, in human gore imbued." The last two lines of the second stanza shows the bloody mess of the snake's fangs, while the angels cry with terror.

"Out –out are the lights- out all!" So the first line of the third stanza indicates a total darkness or evil. Something bad is about to unravel. "And over each quivering form, the curtain, a funeral pall." This next line is a metaphor that is telling what the snake is doing. It is killing each human, and one by one they are falling. The following line says, "Comes down with the rush of storm" Something comes down quickly and heavily. "The angels, pallid and wan," Which means they are white with shock.

The sixth line says, "Uprising, unveiling affirm." There is uproar, and revealing confirm. "That the play is tragedy, "Man" and its hero, the Conqueror Worm." These last two lines show that humans have weaknesses, while the snake doesn't. Therefore, the snake wins. Temptation wins Adam and Eve and they fall to their deaths.

Another poem by Edgar Poe that I will analyze personally is "To Helen," which is about the love he felt for a woman. "Helen, thy beauty is to me," in the first line, shows the beauty of this mysterious woman. "Like those way worn wanderer bore, to his own native shore." It is a metaphor, saying that Helen brought happiness and joy back to Edgar's life after all the pain he suffered. He lost many valuable people and opportunities in his life. If he only had his mother and father, for he will be joyful. If he didn't drop out of college, he could've received a good job. If he didn't miss the meeting, it would've changed his life forever. The job he wanted had disappeared, along with the rest of his dreams. Edgar Allen Poe's tragic life is one many of us are thankful for today. His immense pain, that still scars him for the rest of his life until death, was an ingredient in the creation of amazing, heart-felt poetry.

As the poem continues, the second stanza starts with, "On desperate sees long won't to roam, thy hyacinth hair, thy classic face." Edgar thinks this woman has beautiful hair, and perhaps not a pretty, but distinguished face. Edgar is seeming to describe his love, Virginia Clemms. She was Poe's wife and married when she was only thirteen. Virginia is a family cousin of Poe. But he didn't have the money to get an actual wife, and married Virginia instead.

The next line says, "To the glory that was Greece, and the grandeur that was Rome." Virginia, in this poem, is being compared to Helen of Troy, which was in Greece. Helen was told to be very eloquent and a heroic figure, a beauty. Virginia is also very important to Poe.

"Lo! in you brilliant window- niche." In line eleven is a metaphor showing praise. Virginia looks more mature than her actual age. Edgar adores her. During his life, when Virginia became ill, Poe was extremely stressed, and filled with sorrow. He drank more, even though it didn't help. It shows the love and affection towards her. His wife was everything to him.

"How statues likes see thee stand." In line is indicating that Virginia doesn't sag like and old woman, and has a straight, good posture. "The agate lamp within thy hand." So this emphasizes that she is filled with youth, and indeed very young. "Ah, Psyche, from the regions which, are Holy Land!" This last line of the poem is describing Virginia as a goddess to express her inner and outer beauty, and she is holy to him. But sadly, due to poverty, Virginia died very young, with tuberculosis.

Edgar Allen Poe's poem "The Raven" was the most famous poem throughout his life, and I will provide my own analysis of it using poetry sound devices. "The Raven" is an intricate poem that shows the powerful sounds in poetry. Poe uses mutes and semivowels effectively to emphasize the evil environment, fear in the mind, and weakness of the body.

Mutes and semivowels have all consonances. The mutes are b, d, k, p, q, t and c and g hard. Three of them k, c, and g sound very similar. The semivowels are f, h, j, l, m, n, r, s, v, w, x, y, z, and c and g soft. Semivowels break up into aspirates and liquids. The aspirates are c, f, g, h, j, s, and x, also called strong breath. The liquids are l, m, n, and r because of their fluency of sound. Poe uses these sounds plenty of times throughout this poem.

The first line of the poem says "Once upon a midnight dreary, while I ponder, week and weary," This line has "c" in "once and an" a "p" in upon. Then it says midnight dreary. This part emphasizes the mutes. Midnight has an m and a n, while there is a d in dreary. The second line says, "I ponder, weak and weary," There are semivowels and mutes. The semivowel is the w in weak and weary. The p is a mute, found in the word "ponder." So far, this poem seems as though the semivowels are particularly important. These long semivowels describe the tired state of Poe, both physically and mentally.

The fourth line explains that someone is at the door. The line says, "As of some one gently rapping, rapping at my chamber door." What stands out in this line are the mutes, such as the p and g in the word "rapping." The p and g help the word "rapping" so it sounds like harsh, bitter word. And rapping is usually hard and short. The mutes help create an image in our heads, to hear how a rapping sounds like. Unlike a knock, rapping sounds louder, as readers say the word.

The next line says, "'Tis some visitor,' I muttered, 'tapping at my chamber door.'" This line has semivowels and mutes. The letter "v" as in "visitor" is an example of a semivowel. The mutes are t, p and d. The word with mutes are muttered, tapping, and door. The mutes make the words sound harsher, and not as flowing as the liquids and semivowels.

The second stanza explains the poet's sorrow, his beloved Lenore, now lost forever. The seventh line describes the setting of where he felt deep pain and how his heart was depicted.

"Ah, distinctly I remember it was in the bleak December." He felt tragic at this particular December. The line has mutes. The "b" and "d" in the words "bleak," "distinctly," and "December." The mutes play the parts of unhappiness and cruelty. And the month December has merry holidays, but as Poe writes, this month is horrible for the poet.

The next stanza explains what happened to Lenore, and this mysterious new visitor. The first line of the stanza reads, "And the silken sad, uncertain rustling of each purple curtain." It is a metaphor; the purple curtains stand for Lenore's death.

As the poem continues, it becomes more intense, and powerful. For example, the fifth stanza explains how the boy repeats his beloved's name, think, *hoping*, it is her who came. Lines twenty eight through thirty say, "And the only word there spoken was the whispered word, 'Lenore! This I whispered, and the echo murmured back the word, 'Lenore!' Merely this, and nothing more." This section of the poem has both mutes and semivowels. These letters, l, m, n, and r, are said softy and longer, unlike mutes. The name "Lenore" has liquids, such as l, n, and r.

Lenore is said softy, and has no mutes, and perhaps this is why perhaps the student can't stand the name, because life for him is harsh and tragic, while her name is the exact opposite. This also shows the environment he is living in. When only an echo answered the poet back, this shows that he is lonely, and has no one else around to keep him company. It shows that everyone ignores him, except for Lenore. And now, she is lost.

The next stanza shows that the student is confused, and doesn't know what or who knocked on his door. The rapping progresses, and becomes louder, more ringing. The first line of the sixth stanza says "Deep into the darkness peering, long I stood there wondering, fearing." This line describes the student's fear and evil environment that he lives in. The mutes and semivowels work together to create the image. The l is a semivowel, or more specifically, a liquid. The l is in long. Another semivowel would be the f in the word "fearing." The mutes in this line are d, p and t. The t is in the word "stood" and "there." The d's are particularly important, and helps portray the poet's view of his life so far, after a dramatic death. The letter is in darkness, and deep. Both are not forthcoming, and neither sound hardly friendly. They both sound as though it is mysterious, ominous meaning to these words. This line is foreshadowing a dark sense of evil, and trepidation.

The seventh and eighth stanza describes this new visitor. It is an ancient raven, who had come to visit. This raven is here for a significant role, hence the poem's name, "The Raven." One of the lines explains what this black raven is doing. It says "Perched upon the bust of Pallas just above my chamber door- Perched, and sat, and nothing more." It seems as though the raven seems in no hurry, and is sitting next to the door. He is doing nothing and the poet is not aware that something is very off about the situation. Once again, mutes are playing an important position. The p, d, c, and b are in this line. They are all mutes; the words containing them are "perched," "bust," "chamber," and "door." Mutes are not soft and long words, but rather short and brittle. Since the raven symbolizes death, the words that relate to the raven, is not elegant and nice but more menacing and sinister. Ravens are not the friendliest animals, but they have a reputation, not exactly bad, but not so good either.

This has been my interpretation of this poem. But Poe had explained to the readers about what his poem truly means. And the *Town* had published a humanized raven from the Edgar's poem. It stated that it was the face of the poet himself. One writer named Elizabeth Oakes Smith recalled Poe telling her that his poem was "being talked about a great deal," and the audience "evidently took up the allusion."

An English publisher named Fredrick Saunders claimed that Poe thought of going to England, to read his poem in the presence of Queen Victoria, and present her a copy.

Poe sought to give the "Nevermore" a subtly different meaning with each appearance and to steer between straight forward narrative and of the poetic "suggestiveness" he ruled. Essentially, the poem is about a tale of a young student, despondent by the death of his beloved, visited on a "bleak December" night by an "ominous bird." The raven symbolizes the pain and mourning, and never ending remembrance. The situation in this poem is stated as a conflict between forgetting

41

and remembering. The student tries his best to forget about his love, Lenore. He vows not to speak her name ever again. However, the thoughts of Lenore wouldn't stay down. When there is a mysterious tapping on the door, the student suddenly suspects its Lenore, calling out her name. Unfortunately, he promised himself to never speak of the name, but repeats her name a couple of times throughout "The Raven."

Poe uses a lot of antiquated words to keep the past in the present. He dramatizes the student's enthrallment by using repetition, such as "nevermore." He also restated key words, such as "rapping, rapping" "tell me- tell me," "still is sitting, *still is sitting*." The repetition not only improves to render the student's obsession with his loss and abandonment, but his struggles to not become insane.

In his later comments about the poem, he explains that the student's continued questioning of the raven is in part, "impelled by that species of despair which delights in self-torture," (Silverman, p. 240). The student keeps asking not because he believes the raven has an answer, but to obtain the same word "Nevermore" and so receive "the most delicious because the most intolerable of sorrow." Poe's understanding of his poem might reflect his poem "Irene" ("The Sleeper") that the dead rests in peace only if they remain in living memory. If they are forgotten, they would return to the world in fury. "To forget is to incur the guilt of disloyalty and risk reprisal from the betrayed departed" (Silverman, p. 241). In this view of Poe, the student suffers from incapability to prevent remembrance, but his fear of forgetting.

"The Raven" gives us proof that there is no hope of reunion in heaven. When the student asks the raven tell him, "by that God we both adore," whether he shall again clasp

Lenore in "the distant Aidenn," the raven responds simply, "Nevermore."

Comparing this depressing poem to Edgar Allen Poe, it seems to illustrate his own need to remember. The "bleak December" could relate to another December, perhaps the exact one when his mother Eliza Poe died.

At the end of the poem, the student starts to scream at the raven with rage. He says, "Take thy beak from out my heart, and take thy form from off my door." But the sinister bird remains, never flying away again. The raven is a devourer with its beak in the heart, still a painful link to the past. Assumingly, the raven seems to identify Poe himself, telling the readers that those who we have loved who cease to exist will not ever return, and we can never reunite with them in heaven. They will never be forgotten, and even more painful to give up.

Longfellow and Poe

Certainly, Edgar Allen Poe is a great poet, but he did not get along with other poets and literary figures. On February 28, Poe redelivered his lecture in the New York Society Library. His lecture was on "Poets and Poetry of America." This lecture had been a "vehicle" for his hatred at Rufus Griswold. Among their several similarities, both Poe and Griswold tried in their professional lives to work around "personal hostilities." But even if they were friends, Griswold said nothing of liking Poe, only wanting to reprint his works. A week before, a New York publisher reported a conversation with Griswold. Griswold spoke of Poe, telling him horrible stories about him. It made Poe seem notorious. Poe was not new with the idea of smarminess. He declared to Griswold that he had lost a valuable friend, from his own foolishness. He assured Griswold that he had wrongly based his criticisms of poets and poetry of America on "the malignant defamation of a mischief maker," and his edited version of his lecture contained no offense to him. Unfortunately, he did not do the same with Henry Longfellow.

The *Mirror* played up Poe's speech, promising "exquisite literary cannibalism" (Silverman, p. 236). He spoke for over two hours in front of three hundred people. Many newspapers recorded a fairly full account of the lecture.

Edgar Poe singled out American poets, including the Davidson sisters of New York, "popular sentimental poets whose acclaims he attributed to their both having died in their teens" (Silverman, p. 237). Poe, during the lecture, treated Longfellow in relation to the pantheon (Bryant, Halleck, Sprague, and Dana) whose engravings decorated the frontispiece of Poets and Poetry. Poe extolled the poet highly, but said about Longfellow, "his fatal alacrity at imitation made him borrow when he had better at home" (Silverman, p.237).

But Poe went farther than that. Some newspapers exclaimed that Poe had insulted Longfellow in a discreditable way. The critic from *Boston Atlas* came up with another pun on Poe's name, in which the Boston Reviewers had treated David Poe nearly forty years ago. The critic said that he preferred a "dancing dog...to the man who uttered such remarks...in reference to the poetry of Sprague and Longfellow. It was to come before a Boston audience with such stuff; they would *poh* at him at once" (Silverman, p.237). Poe became infamous all around New York City. But he reached a whole new level of celebrity with his poem "The Raven."

The ongoing "Longfellow War" distressed Poe's partner employer Briggs. He allowed Edgar to take control of his campaign, not realizing that he would write more than one article. But Poe became obsessed on the matter of plagiarism. Briggs knew too that the poet's constant attack attracted the *Journal* and gained its readers. But he was worried about the response of Boston and Cambridge over this nonsense. He wished that Longfellow is too good a fellow to take it much to heart.

Longfellow, however, thought that it was a waste of time writing back to Poe. He said, "Too precious to be wasted in street brawls." Lowell of the *Journal* was annoyed by Poe's harsh remarks, especially to Longfellow's young wife. He filed a complaint to Briggs who replied back that it was a "playful" implication to abstract Mrs. L. Briggs, who told Lowell that Edgar's comments were half as bad as he heard Lowell say. Lowell himself considered Longfellow's talent exaggerated.

Poe also published in the *New York Aristidean* a review of an anthology of Longfellow's poems. Poe wrote defending Longfellow, and wrote anonymously defending himself. This review is actually unclear who had written it, but there is proof that it could have belonged to Poe. It matched the way he wrote, and specific words such as "purloining." It was the cruelest review (if it was him) that he ever wrote.

Longfellow on the other hand, infuriated, excluded Poe from his anthology. Even though he admired and liked Poe's "The Haunted Palace," he said that Poe was the rudest literary thief.

Poe found his financial situation unchanged by his fourteen hour day and the fame of "The Raven." He claimed that while he gained no money, Longfellow had tons. Poe sought to assume that his rightful place in the world and avenge himself against destiny.

Edgar Allen Poe hated Henry Wadsworth Longfellow because Longfellow had a great, fun life and wrote about his happy life, such as found in his poem "The Children's Hour." He uses the power of letters to help portray an image inside the reader's mind.

I will now personally analyze this poem:

Assonances are vowels that repeat in sentences and consonances are consonants that could be repeated and both do not matter where the letter is. It could be in the middle, or end.

At the beginning, the first line says, "Between the dark and the daylight." This line has alliteration, which are the d's in dark and daylight. So the time this poem took place is around dawn. The next line says, "When the night is beginning to lower, comes a pause in the day's occupations." This next line has consonances, the n's in night and in beginning. "Comes a pause in the days occupations." The c is a consonance, and it is found in occupation and comes. This is known as the children's hour.

The second stanza explains how Longfellow hears his daughters wake up and their footsteps. The second line of the second stanza says "The patter of little feet." The consonance is t, found in patter, little, and feet. The third stanza describes his daughters, Grave Alice, and laughing Allegra, and Edith with golden hair. The a's are assonances, such as Alice, laughing, and Allegra.

The fourth stanza tells the readers that the young girls are planning an attack together in line fifteen. It says "They are plotting and planning together." There is alliteration and consonance. The alliteration would be the p's in plotting and planning, and the consonances are the n's in planning and the t's in plotting.

The following stanza portrays a raid that the girls planned. "A sudden from the stairways." This line has alliteration. The s in sudden and stairway are examples of alliteration. The third and fourth line in the fifth stanza says "By three doors left unguarded, they enter my castle wall!" These two lines refer to a metaphor. His castle walls are actually the walls of his studies.

The next stanza describes the daughters on top of their father. In line twenty one, it reads "They climb into my turret." Longfellow creates another metaphor. The turrets are actually just the legs of Longfellow, has the girls climb into it. He calls his legs turrets to show the readers that the girls thought they were very long. The next line says "If I try to escape, they surround me." It is imagery, as if an army is enclosing Longfellow, though he has only three girls.

"Their arms about me entwined," in the seventh stanza has consonance. The t's in about and entwined. In line twenty seven, it states "Till I think of the Bishop of Bingen." There is an assonance, the i as in think, till, Bishop and Bingen.

The eighth stanza explains that the girls are like bandits. "Do you think O blue eyed banditti, because you have scaled the wall." "Scaled the wall," is another metaphor for climbing all over him. This stanza is very playful and joyful.

"I have you fast in my fortress," in line thirty three is a metaphor, and alliteration. The fortress is actually just his room. He called it his fortress maybe because of the size of the room, since he is rich. The f's in fast and fortress is alliteration. It seems that throughout his poem, he uses alliteration consonances, and assonances to create a catchy and rhythmic tune. "But put you down into the dungeons." This is on line thirty five and has consonances and alliteration. The d's in dungeon and down, and the t's are consonances such as found in the words "into," and "put." The next line says, "The round tower of my heart, And there I will keep you forever, Yes forever and a day." He tells the readers he will always keep his daughters in his heart. "Till the walls shall crumble into ruin, and moulder in dust away!" These last two lines of the poem has consonances such as the l's in till, walls, shall, and crumble. Longfellow shows that he loves his daughters, and always will, until the very end and turns into dust.

Bibliography

Meyers, Jeffrey. *Edgar Allan Poe: His Life and Legacy*. New York: Cooper Square Press, 2000.

Oliver, Mary. *A Poetry Handbook*. San Diego: Harcourt Brace & Company, 1994.

Silverman, Kenneth. *Edgar A. Poe: Mournful and Never-ending Remembrance*. New York: Harper, 1992.

"Periodontal Diseases"
Nick Choi

The human tooth, like many structures in the human body, is complex and intricate. It has several layers and structures, all which serve their unique purposes. The actual tooth however, is only enamel, the hardest substance in the human body, and dentine, calcified tissue that protects nerves in the gum. Of course, to hold the tooth in place, periodontal tissue surrounds the tooth. This tissue, and all its parts, is prone to periodontal disease. Surrounding the tooth is periodontium, tissue that specifically protects and supports the teeth. This tissue's main purpose is to protect the nerves found underneath the dentine in pulp. Failure to maintain oral hygiene leads to gingivitis, which will ultimately jeopardize the gum's health, and its surrounding structures.

Gingivitis, the least destructive periodontal disease, is also the most undiagnosed because of its subtleness. Some do not acknowledge many of the obvious, yet commonly ignored symptoms. In most cases, gingivitis begins with bacterial growth inside a biofilm called plaque. A biofilm is a thin layer of billions of bacterial organisms. Without proper dental hygiene, calculus (or tartar) hardens and becomes plaque. The plaque releases toxins inside the periodontal tissue, creating a wound as the bacteria also irritate the surrounding periodontal tissue. As a natural response, the human body sends blood to the wounds created by toxins, which causes the gums to appear inflamed. When the gingiva becomes inflamed, gaps between the gum and teeth form more gingiva and periodontal pockets, where more plaque and debris will remain.

This growth of microorganisms presents itself in a dark yellow hue, one of gingivitis' most conspicuous symptoms. Other symptoms of gingivitis include receding gums, inflamed gingiva, persistent bad breath in the morning, shiny appearance of the gums, and overly sensitive gums. Signs of even one of these symptoms often suggest that one is at the first stages of gingivitis. Seeking professional care is extremely important in stopping gingivitis from progressing to a more destructive periodontal disease.

In most cases, gingivitis is caused by poor dental hygiene and subsequent plaque formation. There are multiple causes of gingivitis, other than poor dental hygiene. For example, gum disease could be caused by an infection, the side-effects of a medication, smoking, depression, poor nutrition, or part of a different health condition. With the absence of plaque, significant complications of gingivitis are rarer. Nonetheless, one should unconditionally contend gingivitis with precaution.

While gingivitis is not a commonly fatal disease, it can

lead to more dangerous health complications and diseases. Gingivitis specifically describes the inflammation of the gingiva, and if left untreated sometimes progresses to periodontists, a disease of the periodontal ligament, which supports the teeth. Unlike gingivitis, periodontitis can result in bone loss, particularly the alveolar bone found underneath periodontal tissue. This threatening periodontal disease also results in the loss of the adjacent attachment apparatus, which is a part of the periodontal tissue. Losing these two integral parts of the periodontal tissue also compromises the health of a tooth. In fact, periodontitis is the leading cause of adult tooth loss.

Gingivitis, in its self, poses a threat; dying from severe gingivitis is not unheard of. In fact, there have been numerous amounts of research conducted proving a correlation between gum disease and cardiovascular disease. Some experts theorize that bacteria enters one's bloodstream through the gingival pockets where the organisms attach to plaque of coronary arteries. Blockages in these arteries can cause cardiovascular diseases and future heart attacks. A recent study (2004) showed that over 90% of cardiovascular disease patients have suffered from moderate to severe gum disease.

Gingivitis is, luckily for thousands of people in the world, a reversible disease. As the bacteria in plaque are the usual cause of gingivitis, therapy is aimed primarily at reduction of plaque to reduce or eliminate inflammation. Doing so gives the gingiva an opportunity to heal without the threat of infection. Dentists often encourage periodontal maintenance that includes personal and professional care, which is important in preventing recurring inflammation.

There are several methods of reducing the inflammation of the gums: mouth rinses, antibiotics, and medical procedures. Most of the medical procedures are surgeries done to regenerate and reconstruct dead periodontium caused by gingivitis. While not as common as simple root planning/scaling, these surgeries are just as successful in producing healthier gums. Mouth rinses are the easiest method to treat gingivitis, although it is the least consistent. Specialized rinses with low concentrations of folic acids have been proven to reduce the inflammation of gingiva. Antibiotics like doxycycline hyclate and chlorhexidine gluconate have been very effective in reducing the inflammation of gingival tissues. Of all the methods of treating gingivitis, conventional and surgical procedures are the most consistently effective in treating gum disease.

The most conventional way to treat chronic gingivitis is through a procedure called scaling and root planning. This treatment of chronic periodontitis has been accepted as the most effective treatment of periodontal disease. Scaling significantly reduces the inflammation and kills plaque-causing bacteria found in one's teeth and gums. Using handheld periodontal scalers, peridontists remove subgingival calculus. Scaling successfully reduces the inflammation and kills the microbial organisms living in the biofilm of the teeth. Studies show that clinical conditions generally improve following root scaling, while patients with more severe cases do not respond to this treatment.

In the majority of gingivitis cases, scaling reduces the inflammation and kills the microbial organisms living in the biofilm of the teeth. Studies show that clinical conditions generally improve after root planning. If a scaling and root planning procedure is unsuccessful, many periodontists recommend mouth rinses and antibiotics. Specialized mouth rinses and antibiotic treatments, in combination with scaling, are very effective in destroying bacteria and plaque. Although they are usually recommended for only specific cases, these two methods compliment dental hygiene extremely well by ridding the periodontium of calculus, hardened plaque.

Other available surgeries are soft tissue grafts, guided tissue regeneration, and flap surgery. Soft tissue grafts are used to fabricate the lost periodontal tissue and offer support to thin gums. Guided tissue regeneration is a surgical procedure in which an artificial membrane is placed between the inflamed gums and teeth, promoting the growth of gingiva and alveolar bone. Flap surgeries treat gum disease by reducing the size of gingival pockets and thereby limiting the area for bacteria to grow. Sometimes, extreme cases require a gingivectomy, a surgical procedure to remove inflamed gingiva tissue. This procedure's main objective is to reproduce a healthy pair of gums and teeth. While mostly cosmetic, the surgery does have practical uses, as it limits the amount of infected gingiva.

Dentists often use the aforementioned procedures to treat already developed gum disease. However, many children and adults often neglect that the best way to "cure" gingivitis is to prevent it. According to the FDA(Food and Drug Administration 2002), as many as 15%-30% of adults encounter gingivitis and other forms of periodontal diseases some time in their life. This overwhelming statistic is a testament to gingivits' subtleness and its incredible threat to the unprepared. Dental hygiene is extremely important in preventing gingivitis, and should be practiced intently.

Works Cited

Mattila, K. J., M. S. Nieminen, V. V. Valtonen, V. P. Rasi, Y. A. Kesaniemi, S. L. Syrjala, P. S. Jungell, M. Isoluoma, K. Hietaniemi, and M. J. Jokinen. "Association between Dental Health and Acute Myocardial Infraction." *Bmj* 298.6676 (1989): 779-81. Print.

Murray, John J. *The Prevention of Dental Disease*. New York: Oxford UP, 1990. Print.

Pader, Morton. *Oral Hygiene Products and Practice*. New York, NY: Marcel Dekker, 1988. Print.

Snape, David. *What You Should Know about Gum Disease: a Layman's Guide to Fighting Gum Disease*. Overland Park, KS: Toothy Grins Pub., 2008. Print.

"Giotto's Arena Chapel and the Italian Renaissance"

Andrew Mun

Italian Renaissance

The Italian Renaissance opened the path to all renaissances. For Europe, the Italian Renaissance was a cultural change and achievement that began in the 13th century and ended around the 1600's. It was a transition from Medieval to Early Modern Europe. Renaissance was a term used by the historians such as Jacob Burckhardt. Renaissance (*rinascimento*) was not in full effect until the end of the 14th century.

The European Renaissance bloomed in the region Tuscany, in central Italy, and affected the cities, Florence and Siena, the most. Renaissance even had an impact on Rome. The Italian Renaissance peaked as attacks from foreigners created a time called the Italian Wars around the mid 1600's.

The Italian Renaissance was best known for its cultural achievements. Renaissance literature began with Petrarch, a person who created a unique writing style. 15th century writers and vernacular poets contributed significant growth to the Renaissance. Architecture also impacted Italy during the Renaissance period. They made works, such as the Florence Cathedral and St. Peter's Basilica in Rome. The last contribution was the Aldine Press, led by Aldo Manuzio, who created a book that was cheap and in Ancient Greek.

The later Middle Ages, 1300's and forward, had lots of difficulties in parts of Italy. Southern Italy at the time was poorer than the north. The city states were the wealthiest in Europe. The Crusades built trade to the Levant, and the Fourth Crusade destroyed the Byzantine Empire. Italy prospered at much trade, and the city states prospered, for they had rich land, called Po Valley. The Renaissance sparked when historians founded academies in Florence and Venice, and artists of the Renaissance excelled from the Ancients.

Arena Chapel

The Arena Chapel was built by a man named Enrico Scrovegni, who built the chapel in order for people to forget his ancestor's crimes over the decades. The Scrovegni family's job was to lend money at a high interest rate. The church did not like this act of "thieving," and, therefore, hated the Scrovegni family. Many citizens hated them as well. The Arena Chapel, or

Scrovegni Chapel, was created to appease them, and it was located in Padua, Italy. He asked Giotto di Bondone, an exceptional artist to paint the inside walls and panels of the chapel.

Giotto did a magnificent job on the frescoes, or paintings on the walls, about Christ and relating to the church. Giotto's masterpieces in the church were considered a milestone, or big jump, in the evolution of western painting. A theme on one of the frescoes of the Arena Chapel was the painting of Judas being paid for betraying Christ. It has a lot of drama and threat, and is shown by the sinister, dark figure that clutches the shoulders of Judas. The scenes of Judas betraying god unfolded over three tiers, or levels. Another set of paintings were *The Last Judgment,* which included Joachim and Anna, the virgin's parents, the painting *Joachim's Expulsion,* from the temple, and consists of six panels, the last panel which is Joachim and Anna at the golden gate. This shows Giotto's strong emotions.

Other painting such as *Incarnation* and *Infancy of Christ* begins at the channel arch. The life of Christ panels continue down the middle tier, and the themes of *Passion, Resurrection, Ascension* and *Pentecost* also begin at the middle tier. Giotto di Bondone created great frescoes in the Arena Chapel. These paintings all showed lots of human emotions and religious imagery. His work is still respected around the world till this day.

Giotto di Bondone

Giotto di Bondone was born in 1266 or 1267. He was a distinguished Italian painter and architect from Florence in the late Middle Ages. His birth, birthplace, his mentor, and his burial is yet unknown. Giotto was known to be the first of the great line of artists to be a part of the Italian Renaissance. A 16th century biographer, Giorgio Vasari claimed that Giotto was very different from the Byzantine styles, and brought art to life. According to Vasari, Giotto was a shepherd boy, loved by all who knew him. Cimabue, one of the famous painters of Tuscany, (the other name, Duccio) one day saw Giotto's drawing of sheep on a rock. Cimabue noticed that it was remarkably well drawn, so he asked Bondone, the father of Giotto, to let Giotto become his apprentice.

Vasari also stated that Giotto drew a red circle perfectly to show the pope his skills. However, many historians disagree with Vasari's facts, since it would be highly improbable for Giotto to be Cimabue's apprentice, and Vasari showed no evidence to back up his facts. It could have been all allegedly remarked.

When Cimabue went to Assisi to paint frescoes, it might have been possible that Giotto accompanied him to the Basilica of St. Francis. There was controversy about whether Giotto painted the Francis cycle, and several sources, such as Ghiberti and Riccobaldo said that the paintings in the Upper Church was one of Giotto's first works of art by himself. In order to find out whether Giotto di Bondone painted the Upper Church frescoes, in 2002, examinations that compared Giotto's paintings in the Arena Chapel in Padua to the paintings in the church at Assisi showed different results between the two. Therefore, it is unlikely that Giotto did the paintings within the Upper Church.

Giotto was said to have first painted for the Dominicans in the church of Santa Maria Novella, based on Vasari's facts. Giotto painted a fresco of the Annunciation and the enormous suspended *Crucifix*, about five meters high. This was painted around 1290. Before this event in 1287, Giotto, age 20, married

Ricevata di Lapes del Pela. They have quite a large number of children, and one of them, Francesco, became a painter, like his father. Giotto might have worked in Rome from 1297-1300, but not much evidence proves that he was there. The Basilica of St. John Lateran had a fresco painted during this period for the Jubilee of 1300 by Bonface the eighth. Giotto also painted during the period Badia Polyptch novel in Uffizi, Florence.

As Giotto grew, his name became more famous, and he was to work in Padua and Rimini. It is said in documents of 1301 to 1304 that Giotto had big estates in Florence, and probably led a large workshop throughout Italy.

The most famous place for where Giotto displayed his work was at Padua in the Scrovegni, or Arena Chapel. He was hired by the founder Enrico degli Scrovegni to paint there.

Bondone painted everything based on the bible. He painted themes such as the Virgin Mary, and the Last Judgment. Many of his frescoes had a lot of meanings, (37 to be precise) and scholars could not tell which was the most accurate to describe each painting.

Cimabue's style of painting compared to Giotto. Cimabue painted Medieval, while Giotto drew like Arnolfo di Cambio. Unlike the figures seen by Cimabue and Duccio, Bondone's figures did not follow the Byzantine models. They were three dimensional, had faces and gestures, and were dotted in garments. The figures had naturalistic elements, resembling stage sets. Giotto involved his figures in particular ways in scenes, and his human faces were different than his contemporaries. For example, when a soldier took a baby away from its mother in *Massacre of the Innocents*, he had an expression of shame on his face. A 19th century critic John Ruskin said, "He painted the Madonna and St. Joseph and Christ yes, by all means…, but essentially Mama, Papa and Baby."

Giotto's paintings

These are my own analysis of Giotto's frescos:

"Wedding at Cana"

One of the frescos that Giotto di Bondone painted was called *The Wedding at Cana*. This painting is located on the middle row and third wall of the Arena Chapel in Padua. This fresco is basically about Jesus turning water into wine. This painting looks splendidly done, and is very artistic in a religious sense. There are eleven people in the picture, including Jesus Christ. They are all sitting around a table, and it seems to be inside a building with no roof top, and judging by the color painted of the sky, it was around evening to night.

Jesus Christ has the cross around his head, making him an important character in this fresco and, of course, throughout history. This scene looks morose and joyful at the same time. I see people with sad expressions, and those who have a smile playing at their lips. The painting is very accurately painted, and even had shapes around the wedding scene. Off to the side, there is a man who is wearing a cloak, sprouting water from a rock with his baton. The perimeter of this fresco is adorned with detailed patterns, and looked very difficult to plan and paint.

The people in the scene who also have a yellow glow behind them could mean that they play a significant part in the scene and throughout history. The building is drawn without much detail, showing that probably the couples who are getting married are not rich. Off to the side shows servants and a fat man drinking wine that was supposedly made by Jesus by converting it from water. There was a man standing next to the fat man, most likely seeing if the wine was genuine. Probably the man with the stick with gushing water may have a part in this scene too.

I believe the woman who is getting wed is showing a worried expression since all they had was water to give to the high class citizens. Jesus has his hand raised to turn the water into wine. The painting is, in a way, artistically proportionate, especially the designs on the sides and edges of the scene. Overall, this painting is really a piece of advanced and very descriptive art.

"The Resurrection of Lazarus"

Another one of Giotto di Bondone's famous frescoes was *The Resurrection of Lazarus* in the left wall in the Arena Chapel in Padua. In this particular scene, Jesus Christ had raised the mummy, Lazarus, from the dead. These people are all dressed in cloaks, and some of them had veils covering their faces. The people seem to have facial expressions of skeptics since they don't believe this miracle that Jesus had brought back a dead human being to life. Lazarus, is dressed in mummy clothing, and is currently being unclothed in this fresco by a man next to him. In the bottom right corner of the painting, there are two men pushing a coffin away from the scene, supposedly that was Lazarus's coffin.

Jesus Christ is very powerful and influential in this painting since he has a strong and bright yellow glow and a holy cross behind his head, along with people watching him with uncertainty, and others at his feet, begging for his forgiveness, or begging for a favor. Jesus has a hand raised and seems to make the mummy come back to the living world.

There are three others who have a yellow glow behind them. They are the man who is in a tan cloak, untying the mummy Lazarus from his bonds, who also has the glow and a woman with a veil over her mouth. These three characters are coincidentally standing side by side, and must play an important role in this painting. It is night, judging by the dark blue colors in the sky, and people, including Christ are located by a mountain. It seems to be very cold by how everyone wore their clothing.

There seems to be much commotion going on, most likely because an extraordinary phenomenon has happened. That phenomenon was Jesus resurrecting someone back to life. Jesus has a stern and concentrated look on his face, and the people in this fresco avoid standing next to him or directly in front of him. There are a bunch of people, who stand behind him in this scene. This picture is artistically very challenging to paint, and must have taken much practice and precision.

Jesus does not seem to be distinguished from everyone else in this picture, besides the yellow cross behind his head. It seems to be that the people who wear plain colors of clothing, such as green or white, seem to be the lower class, while the upper class has two or more colors of clothing, and some of them cover their faces with veils.

The mummy Lazarus is truly painted accurately for looks as though he were dead, compared to the rest of the civilians. The mummy's eyes have a faraway look, and the eyes are filled with misty blue. Lazarus's face looks pale and gaunt, and the skin is opaque. Clearly Giotto made Lazarus look different from the other people. Giotto used great colors to make the mummy look dead. The pale white on his face and the misty blue eyes really gives us a sense of what a not living person looks like.

There is a group of people behind a man with a green robe, protesting for some reason. It could be to reassure that Jesus has a power that people should not underestimate, or attempt to revolt against Christ. The group is totally ignored. The ground is painted with a mixture of yellow and brown, supposedly they are all on sand.

The main idea of this fresco is that Jesus Christ brought someone back from the dead, but people either don't know how to react and has a look of doubt. One way or another, Jesus has performed one of his very unique powers to the people.

This picture is so old, that there are some fading of paint, scratches or marks and cracks on this fresco. Nevertheless, it is one of the masterpieces that Giotto di Bondone made from the Italian Renaissance that will forever be looked upon with huge religious beliefs, artistic appreciation and pure awe.

"Lamentation"

Lamentation is the name of another fresco that Giotto di Bondone painted around 1306. It is located on the bottom row and left wall of the Arena Chapel in Padua. In this scene, there is a lot of sorrow and tears. Jesus had been crucified and had died. Everyone in the picture, including the angels above, is weeping. Jesus Christ had been the leader that many people looked up to. The person they had all loved dearly, Jesus Christ, is gone. In order to show who Jesus was in this scene, Giotto made him with the yellow cross behind his head. It was glowing brightly, possibly to represent that Jesus Christ was not yet out of the entire picture. He will somehow still be an important character; even though he is currently dead. The people around him have tears or unhappy looks on their faces.

Eight people and the ten angels in the sky have yellow glows behind them, to show that they are all important in this painting. The eight humans are mostly made up of women surrounding Jesus Christ with tears on their faces. The other two men were off to the side, not too close to Jesus Christ as the women, but observing him with sad faces.

The crowd behind a woman with pale pink clothing are all sad also, and have cloaks over their heads, and they all looked face down onto Jesus, with sorrow. The men with the yellow glow around them were holding Jesus with looks of sorrow. A woman with dark blue robes was cradling his head, as if to try and wake Jesus Christ up.

The women in purple and green each held the hands of Jesus Christ, as if he wasn't alone and that they respected him with high esteem. A woman with a dark pink and red dress was holding his feet, examining them with great sadness. Two women, with pink and purple clothing are looking down upon Jesus, to see if he was truly dead. They both are crying.

The scene is filled with sadness, and even the angels are disturbed. They are flying around in the sky with mixed feelings of dread and shock. They had halos behind their heads, and had wings that matched the color of their clothing. These angels all looked like women. Some angels, for example, the one in a pink dress, had hands placed on the side of her face to represent sleep. Possibly, they were telling Jesus to rest in peace, and to sleep peacefully. Other angels had sad expressions of sadness. One angel in a pale yellow dress was using her clothes to wipe the tears from her face. The sky is fragmented into approximately ten parts, and the colors are assorted dark blue, making this night or close to it.

The people and angels are located near a cliff, with a tree that is bare. Usually, bare trees show ominous signs of a bad happening, or danger. In this fresco, it represents that someone important had died. Jesus indeed looks dead from his look into the night sky, his pale white body, and the faceless expression. Jesus Christ showed no sign that he heard what was going on. This was a very important scene in history also, since Jesus having died was a huge incident, since Jesus Christ was the son of Almighty God. The people's clothing is plain robes, and two of the men off to the side has priest-like clothing. They could possibly be priests or Jesus' followers.

The people in plain clothes could have been the poor class. This piece really shows what sadness is about, due to the fact that everyone is sad about the tragic death of Jesus. Giotto has truly done a great work of art. Around the perimeter of the painting are tiles or geometrical shapes that make the fresco look more artistic and less tedious. There is a picture to the left of the fresco which shows a man being eaten by a whale. I have heard this story before at church, and it is about a man who falls into the sea, and is eaten by a whale. Everyone thought he was dead for good, but he was alive and managed to get out of the whale's stomach. There is no obvious relation to *Lamentation,* except that this could foreshadow that Jesus, although thought to be dead, will turn out to be alive and well as the man in the whale did. Jesus did indeed come back to the living world after three days. Yet, this doesn't happen until afterword.

Jesus Christ was a religious leader to many. It was tragic that he was crucified. Giotto di Bondone portrayed a morose atmosphere with all the sad expressions on the humans' and angels' faces and the bare tree. Giotto had truly outdone himself. This fresco shows his artistic personality, and even though he painted these at a young age, his pictures are all professional. This is another great piece of artwork by the famous Giotto di Bondone.

Giorgio Vasari

Giorgio Vasari was born on July 30th, 1511. He was a skilled Italian painter, writer, historian and architect, who is lauded today because of his biographies on Italian artists, which are considered a foundation of art-historical writing.

Giorgio Vasari was born in Arezzo, Tuscany. He was sent to a skilled painter of stained glass named Guglielmo da Marsigla. He became a student of this painter, and at the age of sixteen, he joined the circle of Andrea del Sarto in Florence. Andrea's pupils were Rosso Fiorentino and Jacapo Pontormo. This was where Giorgio's humanist education was encouraged. Vasari was influenced by the painting styles of Michelangelo, who even became his friend.

Giorgio Vasari came to Rome and learned about Raphael and other Roman High Renaissance in 1529. His own Mannerist paintings were ironically more appreciated while he lived than after his death. In 1547, Giorgio finished the hall of chancery in Palazzo della Cancelleria in Rome with frescoes that were named Sala dei Cento Giorni. He kept being called to work particularly in the Medici family in Florence and Rome. Vasari worked in many places. Some of them included Arezzo and Naples.

One of the most important pictures Giorgio Vasari ever completed was the wall and ceiling painting of the great Sala di Cosimo The First. It was located in the Palazzo Vecchio located in Florence. This was where in 1555, his work on the frescoes started in the cupola of the Duomo. It was completed by Ederico Zuccari with Giovani Balducci.

Giorgio Vasari was actually more successful as an architect rather than a painter. His loggia of the Palazzo degli Uffizi next to the Arno River was a great work of architecture. The loggia along with the Vasari Corridor goes next to the Arno River, crosses the Ponte Vecchio, and goes around the exterior of several buildings. Another work of architecture was when Vasari renovated the churches of Santa Maria Novella and Santa Croce, and some of the changes and improvements he did was remodeling the retro choir. A piece of High Renaissance architecture was when Vasari made an octagonal on top of the Basilica of Our Lady of Humility in Pistoia. As one can see, although Giorgio Vasari was well known for his magnificent frescoes, architecture was his main priority.

Giorgio Vasari did a considerable amount of work during his lifetime, which included working in Rome at Pope Julius The Third's Villa Giulia, along with Giacomo Barozzi da Vignola and Bartolomeo Ammanati, and a grand home in Rome. The home was adorned with paintings all over the walls and vaults. It is now currently a museum. He was very wealthy, and rose from part of the priori, or a municipal council of his native town.

Giorgio Vasari in 1563 assisted in the founding of the Accademia e Compagnia delle Arti del Disegno, an art academy in Florence. The leaders of this academy were the Grand Duke and Michelangelo, which had control over the members of the institution, which at the time had 36 artists. Vasari died 11 years after the founding of the institution in Florence on June 27th.

Known as one of the first Italian art historians, Vasari used the term 'rinascita', which meant Renaissance, numerous times. He published a book in 1550 called, *Lives of the Most Eminent Painters, Sculptors and Architects*, dedicated to the

Grand Duke Cosimo I de' Medici. This was a highly valued treatise on technical methods used in art, which was rewritten in 1568, and included woodcut portraits of artists.

Vasari's work was in favor of Florentines, and Venetian art was ignored in the first edition. Giorgio then traveled to Venice and created the 2nd edition, which was also on a specific point of view.

Many historians both back in Giorgio's day and in the modern world wondered if his facts in his biographies were truly correct. Some facts were absolutely valid, while others seemed guessed or lied. Overall, most of his work seemed inaccurate since he provided no dates. Only painters of his day and of the past would follow Vasari's beliefs. Modern criticism has corrected Vasari's facts, yet his work is considered to be a splendid.

Competition was a word that Giorgio Vasari used, according to Richard Goldthwaite, and he used competition in an economical sense. Just like when Giorgio described Florentine artists, who progressed since they wanted much competition. Vasari claimed that competition is, "one of the nourishments that maintain them."

Giotto di Bondone: the Arena Chapel Frescoes

Giotto was a revered and special figure during the Renaissance period, and even after his death, he was still legendary. The question is, why did he become so famous and how did he pave the path from other painters to follow.

The best art pieces by Giotto are all in the Arena Chapel in Padua. These paintings were all made during his early life, and yet they show true qualities of a professional painter.

According to the author James Stubblebine, Giotto di Bondone was born in Colle di Vespignano, a village near Florence, around 1267. James Stubblebine claimed that Giotto was most certainly an apprentice of Cimabue, the most lauded painter of the generation before. Vasari states in page 71 that Cimabue found Giotto when he was drawing sheep on a rock. Giotto's work looks different than that of Cimabue's since Giotto had some experience or other types of traditions, such as the Roman fresco painting style and French Gothic sculpture. Out of these styles, Giotto made a new one, which had caused Dante to write in his famous lines in Purgatorio. "Cimabue thought that in painting ... He commanded the field, and now Giotto has the acclaim..." (Stubblebine, pg. 71)

We don't know much of Giotto's *oeuvre* (art work), despite his clarity in his artistic personality. A lot of critics are saying how young Giotto had connection to the St. Francis church at Assisi. Though the works in the Arena Chapel and the Upper Church of St. Francis have some resemblances, they both have a different approach.

James Stubblebore says that there is no document of commission that has been saved, and the earliest references related to Giotto working at the Arena Chapel is a list of his paintings written down between 1312 and 1318 by Riccobaldo Ferrarese. A description of Giotto's figure of Envy written in between 1308 and 1312 was by Francesco da Barberino. There has been no doubt over the centuries that the frescoes were of Giotto's own. These frescoes represented his maturity over the years.

In 1300, Enrico Scrovegni of Padua purchased a piece of land from the Dalesman Family, and the land included the Roman Arena. Around the perimeter of the arena, Enrico built a palace, which was his family home. The reason why people call the chapel the Arena Chapel is because it was built over a Roman Arena.

Next to the palace, Enrico Scrovegni built a chapel dedicated to the Virgin of Annunciation, Santa Maria, and Annunziata. Enrico's family was rich due to his father, Reginaldo, who did usury to technically rob people of money. There is strong proof in showing that Enrico built the Arena Chapel to erase his father's sins. There were two documents which stated two different dates about when the permission was granted to erect the chapel. One document says it was before March 1st, 1302, while another says the March of 1303.

In March, 1304, Pope Benedict granted permission to those suited "Santa Maria del Carita de Arena" in Padua. It is also said that the chapel, built by Scrovegni, was also to dedicate the Virgin of Charity, an appropriate choice since his family had cheated and hoarded money with usury.

James Stubblebine states that evidence that the chapel was property consecrated on March 25, 1305, on the Feast of the Annunciation. Another document tells of the monks who had a church nearby, and they complained that Enrico had made the chapel so that it could be worshipped by his family members. "I find this amusing since Enrico Scrovegni seems to be an unselfish person. Either Enrico has a hidden secret he does not want to say or the monks are stating lies." (Stubblebine, pg. 73)

The Annunciation had been featured for many years in front of a chapel, with two boys dressed up as the angel Gabriel and the Virgin Mary. These performances, according to the author, took place around as early as 1278. As strange as this may seem, Giotto was never documented in the documents of the Arena Chapel. "Even thought Giotto was the main reason for the church to be famous, it is unusual to see him out of the written records. Perhaps back then, his frescoes weren't that well known or appreciated." (Stubblebine, pg. 73) Some visitors of 1304 suggested that Giotto had painted in the chapel for as early as 1303. We suppose that Giotto finished his paintings around 1305.

It is sad according to James Stubblebine that some critics thought Giotto was called in after the months by Enrico due to the monk's complaints for a simpler, broader scheme. Giotto di Bondone represented simpler art works to placate the monks, and the paintings took around 1305 to 1310. However, the pictures shouldn't be called any simpler than Giotto's other paintings. They are all still colorful and decorated almost everywhere. Would this still have been a popular art location if Giotto hadn't painted those pictures? The author, James Stubblebine is still unsure. "I believe that it still would have been a popular art attraction for tourists and art lovers since Giotto di Bondone still made remarkable piece of paintings, and was yet a famous painter throughout time." (Stubblebine, pg. 74)

The Arena Chapel is unusually very plain on both the outside and the inside. There is nothing special about the designs of the chapel, and can be overlooked by many people. The only reason why this chapel stood out during the Renaissance and centuries later was the fact that Giotto di Bondone decorated the entire chapel with amazing frescoes, making up for the plainness of the inside of the tiny church. The windows were all on the south wall and not on the north side, supposedly to help make the pictures be seen clearer through the south wall of the chapel, illuminating the frescoes. James Stubblebine called the Arena Chapel "the viewing box," since the frescoes were easily seen when the windows were all on the south side.

Giotto di Bondone wanted his flow of pictures to show a story, with frescoes going in event order. These paintings went from left to right, and they started at the south wall to the north wall, with three bands. Each band represented a different story. The top band showed the scenes from the Virgin's parents, Joachim and Anna. The middle to lower bands was the topic of "The life and Passion of Christ." Underneath those two bands are the six Virtues and the six Vices. The triumphal arch contains a rendition of the Annunciation. The west wall has the theme, "The Last Judgment."

On the top band, are the scenes of Joachim and Anna. Since Giotto could not use the New Testament, he used apocryphal writings and popular stories which filled in the gaps in the Gospel. Giotto most likely used the book, *The Golden Legend*, by Jacobus de Voragine, and was published in the middle of the 1300's.

In the first scene of the story, Joachim is expelled from the temple of Jerusalem, since he offered a lamb. It was a wrong act of doing since the old couple was childless, and only people who had children could sell the lamb. In the fresco, Joachim is thrown from the temple, looking quite embarrassed. Ironically, a young man who was a bystander secretly got in with permission. "Joachim should not be treated this way, yet this could be an important part of becoming the parents of the Virgin, so not all is lost." (Stubblebine, pg. 76)

In the second scene, Joachim is walking by the countryside, and looks confused about where to go. Local shepherds completely ignore him, even though the dogs are barking at Joachim. He is lost, but not for long.

In the third scene, Anna is praying to help find her husband. This scene takes place in the couples' home, and is unusually painted with lots of detail, though the idea is to contrast the homelessness of Anna's home, to Joachim's vigil. Since Anna was alone, an angel from God came to her, and told her that she was to bear a child and that God will favor her. God chose Anna specifically for this honor, and Anna listens sharply as the angel explains in a carefree voice. A servant in the picture was on the porch, trying to hear what was going on.

The next fresco comes back to Joachim. He sacrificed animal bones in an altar, which earned the favor of God, who appears in the sky. The next painting shows Joachim sleeping and an angel in his vision says that Joachim will have a child named Mary, who will be the mother of the Most High. At the end of the speech, the angel tells Joachim to go back and meet Anna at the Golden Gate. Some shepherds tending their flocks are working under the dark sky, and one Sheppard looks up to the sky, and judging by the color, and the clothing of the shepherds suggest that it is night.

The reunion of Joachim and Anna is by far the most famous out of all reunions. They both meet at the Golden Gate, and hug each other in relief. On-lookers in this fresco includes young women, who were gazing at the old couple, and another woman, who was staring at them through a veil, so hopefully they wouldn't notice her. Giotto displays a great example of how humans react to events.

What began as a dark scene of Joachim being expelled became a happy reunion, and they also showed God's powers and how capricious he is about choosing his favored ones. It could have been anyone, but God chose Joachim and Anna, and changed their lives for the better.

The selected scenes in this particular story had great transition with a lot of religious and artistic meanings. However, these paintings were not necessarily all important. The fresco where Joachim was walking in the country could have been replaced with a more important scene, such as Joachim giving Allas. Nevertheless, Giotto's narration was an exceptional work of art and skill.

After this story, there is a picture of a gate that could allow a reader to adjust to another story with time, and start a new chapter on the next wall, which is The Life of The Virgin. "It is a useful idea to make someone realize that the story ended by visualizing anything that takes up space like a gate. It's a barrier that a spectator sees, which gives them some time to get ready for another story." (Stubblebine, pg 77)

The Life of The Virgin makes up of six panels. They are, *The Birth of the Virgin* takes place on the east side of the triumphal arch, and the setting goes back to Anna's bedroom, where the servants are bathing the baby Virgin. The next fresco is called *The Presentation of the Virgin in the Temple*, where the couple and the Virgin see a temple where a priest takes the Virgin in to live in a new home.

These four scenes all revolve around the betrothal of the Virgin. The scene is from *The Mating of the Rods*, where men who want to marry the Virgin place their rods on an altar in a temple. The expectation on the men's faces is very evident, and for a couple of scenes, the people wait for a sign, which is the rod bursting into flowers on which a dove decides to rest upon. Then the person who brought the rod will be the victor. Joseph was actually the winner of the event. He thought he was too old, and at first doesn't decide to show up. When he finally did, the rod changed into flowers. The last scene is called *The Virgin's return*, where the Virgin prepares for the wedding, and Joseph goes back to Bethlehem to prepare also. Although it ends here, the story shows us the experiences and situations that are within this narration.

In the Annunciation, which starts at the triumphal arch, is a very important story. God gives a message to Gabriel, the angel who sends it to the Virgin. She is ready to receive this message. On the bottom of these paintings, Giotto inserts two more episodes called, *The Pact of Judas* on the left, and *The Visitation* on the right.

The Life of Christ consists of four cycles. They are, The Infancy cycle, The Mission or teaching cycle, Passion cycle, and the Resurrection cycle. These four cycles that Giotto chose were from the popular legends, called Nativity. Even though the Scripture didn't refer to an ox and ass, it was a tradition where the ox stood for the New Testament, and the ass stood for the Old Testament.

Giotto's Nativity was basically the same concepts. Yet the changes Giotto did were startling. He omits the cave in the background in the painting of the grotto in Bethlehem, where Christ was born. This cave was also known for where Jesus was placed in after he died. *The Golden Legend* by Voragine said that Nativity took place in the shed or a shelter against to uncertainties of the weather. Giotto had a picture of the Virgin and Christ in a shed open to the elements on all sides. Giotto also refers to the traditional episode, or subplot of the first bath of Jesus. Two maids bathed him, which was supposed to represent the rite of baptism. Giotto probably changed the traditional iconographic details, according to James Stubblebine, such as the bath of Jesus, to make a high dramatic tone for his painting that was above what the earlier traditions and painters did. The Virgin seems to be staring at Christ with a morose expression, most likely because she is looking into the future, and knows of Christ's fate.

In the narrative *The Pieta*, Giotto shows the Virgin and dead Christ in such a particular way, that therefore a spectator would recall The Nativity, where the Virgin gives Jesus to a servant. "If the painting was that strong, Giotto must have put a lot of emotion into the piece. The painting must be very significant." (Stubblebine, pg. 82)

In the second scene, *The Adoration of the Magi*, takes place in the same setting as The Nativity, except the Virgin is involved. Traditional folklore is involved in many of the pieces. The three Magi are Gasper, Balthasar, and Melchior. In *The Golden Legend*, Voragine, claims that each of the Magi's gifts were symbolic in meaning. Gold was for proper royalty, frankincense was incense to divine worship, and the myrrh, used for the burial of the dead. Voragine says that the Magi were not Jewish, but still came to worship Christ, posing a threat to Herod Antipas, tetrarch of Galilee.

In *The Presentation of Christ in the Temple*, Jesus is supposed to be brought to the priest in a temple, and in order to get him back, the parents must give the priest two white doves. Joseph holds the doves in order to get Jesus back. Anna and Simeon saw the scene. The Virgin shows her humbleness and proves that Christ had not come to destroy the Jewish law, but to complete it.

The next fresco, *The Flight to Egypt* is a scene of terror. Herod had issued an order to kill all males less than two years of age in attempt to kill Christ. Everyone is running, and an angel is pointing in a direction. The Virgin hides Jesus so he won't be killed.

In *The Massacre of the Innocents*, the painting is filled with despair, and horror. With this scene, Giotto finishes the cycle of Christ's Infancy. On the middle row of the opposite wall is the cycle of teaching or mission of Christ's life. In the first scene, twelve year old Jesus talks to elders, displaying his wisdom and intelligence. The Virgin and Joseph scold him, yet Christ merely says, "I must be about my Father's business."

Jesus' greatest deeds were in the frescoes, *The Marriage at Cana*, and *The Resurrection of Lazarus*. In, the *Marriage at Cana*, Jesus displays his powers by turning the water at the feast into wine. He showed the same power at *The Last Supper*, where Jesus mixed his own blood into wine. *The Resurrection of Lazarus i*s when Jesus brings Martha and Mary Magdalen's brother back to life. This scene relates to Christ when he himself rose from the dead. To represent the relations, Giotto puts the *Resurrection of Christ* below the scene of Lazarus.

In The Entry into Jerusalem, Christ shows that he is God's instrument, And that Jesus Christ will willingly accept his fate. In the fresco, people are making a path for Jesus and they are displaying their garments to him, beside a donkey that Christ is riding on.

The painting of entry could either conclude the mission of Christ or begin the cycle of Passion. Before Passion is the scene where Jesus expels all the merchants who sacrifice animals to a temple. The fresco is called *The Expulsion of the Merchants from the temple.*

In the Mission cycle Christ has a new posture, is facing right with his hand raised. This intensity varies from scene to scene.

In the Cana episode, Jesus raises his hand in a sort of sleight of hand way. In the Baptism, it is defined as acceptance, in the Lazarus scene it is known as a command of miracle working, in the entry it is a blessing and greeting, and in the Expulsion it is denunciation. "Jesus Christ's raised hand is interpreted in many different ways, as one can see. However, they all represent one thing; Jesus has the power to do anything, no matter how challenging the task" (Stubblebine, pg. 85) This posture is repeated thoroughly throughout the frescoes, signifying Christ's fate.

The pictures come back to the triumphal arch, and there is an episode that links the next row of scenes below. The scene is called *The Pact of Judas*, which is across *The Visitation.*

The Visitation is about the Virgin and Elizabeth, conversing without any evil, where in *The Pact of Judas*, a sinister dark figure is clutching Judas, creating mass evil. This is why these two paintings are on the opposite walls of each other. This scene is to show sinfulness and wrongdoing committed by most of the Scrovegni family, Judas, and the merchants from *The Expulsion of the Merchants from the Temple*. These people all have a common sin; greediness. The Scrovegni family used usury to become rich, Judas received thirty silvers for an evil job, and the merchants were greedy for money. "Giotto showed all spectators how sins are life scars forever, and committing them are not the right way to live." (Stubblebine, pg. 85)

Down the south wall are the five pictures of the Passion cycle: *The Last Supper, The Washing of the Feet, The Betrayal of Christ, Christ before Caiaphas*, and *The Mocking of Christ*. The Last Supper took place on the feast of Passover, and it was when Jesus told the disciples that one of them betrayed him. The bread and wine, Christ explained that they stood for his body and his blood, for the remission of sins. Giotto raises the drama as the story continues in the Passion cycle in *The Washing of the Feet*. Jesus is setting an example for the disciples within this painting. *The Betrayal of Christ* is a chaotic scene, with everyone out to arrest Jesus. Christ is in a yellow robe to represent a traitor. The story continues down to Christ before the high priest Caiaphas, which shows Jesus; melancholy face about the world, and Caiaphas' rage.

In *The Mocking of Christ*, Christ is dressed in a purple robe, given a rod to represent a scepter, and has a crown of thorns on his head. The soldiers mock him by crying, "Hail, the king of Jews!"

The passion cycle goes to the north all in the string of frescoes: *The Road to Calvary, The Crucifixion, The Pieta*, and *The Pentecost*. Compared to other scenes, the low drama is in *The Crucifixion,* and *The Road to Calvary. The Crucifixion* shows the soldiers watching Christ, with St. John and the Virgin crying in sorrow. In the center, is Jesus Christ, who is not responding.

After this unhappy event comes another one with even more grief. *The Pieta* shows two men off to the side, Nicodemus and Joseph of Arimathea; they are the least emotional out of the group. The Virgin is cradling Jesus' head, and at the feet of Christ is Magdalen, who is crying heavily. Above her is St. John, who expresses his grief by stretching his arms out wide with a facial expression of horror.

The Resurrection is made up of two parts; on the left, the angel who is a witness of *The Resurrection*, and Christ and Magdalen together at the right. *The Resurrection* could be shown by the Three Martyrs, who were the ones announced by an angel that Christ resurrected. Instead, Giotto made Mary Magdalen the first witness of Christ's resurrection.

Christ went to heaven after forty days of seeing his disciples; this was called, *The Ascension*. We see Christ rising up to the sky, ascending to heaven. After Giotto, *The Ascension of Christ* and *The Assumption of the Virgin* were the most popular representations in the late 14th century painting.

The last and final scene is *The Pentecost*. Apostles are gathered together, and the Holy Spirit comes down and gives them each the ability to speak many different languages. Giotto di Bondone ends the story, with the apostles ready to teach about the Church.

The lowest part of the nave walls are decorated with the painted Virtues and Vices. Both groups are opposite sides of each other; The Vices on one side, and the Virtues on the opposite. These figures are all painted the same way so that none will stand out. These figures are there to show the contrasts between each Virtue and its' Vice. Hope is floating up, while Despair is sagging down. As one can see, this is one contrast.

All the Vices are imperfect; they are negative and disorderly. Inconstancy is shown out of control on a disk, yet it's opposite, Fortitude is easy balance, sturdy and decisive. Justice is crowned and enthroned, with each hand holding figures that represent Justice. The opposite of Justice is Injustice, like robbery and wrongdoing.

Infidelity is off balance, and it is following things that everyone believes though it is not right. The opposite of Infidelity is all faithful compared to Infidelity. Wrath is angry, and is tearing her garment, while Temperance is calm, and graceful. "Giotto had made very unusual and unique paintings of these figures." (Stubblebine, pg. 89)

The gigantic *Last Judgment* takes up the entrance wall on the west end of the Arena Chapel. Unlike most scenes, *The Last Judgment* is a theme. It is the contrasts between the Saved and the Damned, the representation of Jesus being the Judge of the World, and the orderly rulings of celestial beings. *The Last Judgment* all together is a mixed theme with overwhelming series of beliefs.

Giotto's main benefactor to *The Last Judgment* was the one in the Baptistry in Florence, which supposedly he knew ever since childhood. From that mosaic, Giotto probably took the posture of Christ, his right hand up in acceptance to the Saved, and the left hand in rejection top those Damned. There are indefinitely differences between *The Last Judgment* on Florence and Giotto's. It is that the one in Florence was old Italo-Byzantine, compared to Giotto's Christ, who is more human, and represents Greater sternness in Baptistry.

The Last Judgment emphasized on the consequences of usury. Giotto may have made it for the Scrovegni family. Unusually, the Virgin is involved in the Arena Chapel frescoes. Ordinarily, she is by the right side of Christ. The Virgin seems to be the head of the Saved.

Bibliography

Lowis, Kristina, and Tamsin Pickeral. *50 Paintings You Should Know*. New York: Prestel Pub, 2009.

Stubblebine, James H. *Giotto: The Arena Chapel Frescoes*. New York: W. W. Norton & Company, 1996.

Wolf, Norbert. *Giotto Di Bondone: 1267-1337*. New York: Taschen, 2006.

"남수단의 미래-발전 가능성을 중심으로"

Kevin Jung

2011 년 7 월 9 일, 무더운 여름날 남수단의 800 만 주민은 총을 내려놓고 눈물을 흘리며 환호했다. 세계에서 가장 긴 전쟁으로 기록된 50 년 내전으로 30 만 명의 사상자를 낸 끝에 마침내 남수단의 평화독립이 선언된 것이다. UN 에 힘입어 무려 98.8%의 찬성표를 얻어 북수단으로부터 독립한 남수단은 기나긴 전쟁의 후 폭풍에도 불구하고 무엇이든 할 수 있다는 자신감에 차있다. 아프리카의 신생독립국인 남수단이 앞으로 발전하기에 어떤 잠재력을 가지고 있는지 살펴본다.

남수단과 대한민국 (같은 점)

남수단의 현 상황은 마치 한국의 1950 년대와 비슷하다. "3 만 1,707 명의 어린이 중 절반이 영양실조이고, 30%인 9,013 명은 아예 학교를 나오지 못한다" (조선일보, 1957 년, 5 월 23 일자 4 면). 『대한민국을 즐겨라』라는 책에서는 이 구절을 "아프리카 어느 나라 이야기가 아니다." (p.27, 정경민) 라고 설명한다. 50 년 전의 남한과 현재의 아프리카는 마치 거울을 보듯이 비슷한 모습을 하고 있다. 먹고 살기도 힘든 현실, 땅은 전쟁의 후 폭풍으로 오염되어있고, 사람들은 교육을 받지 못해 도적질이나 싸움질을 일삼으며 삶을 연명한다. 하지만 한국의 성공사례를 접한 남수단의 현 대통령 살바 키이르는 한국의 새마을 운동을 롤모델로 삼아 남수단을 부흥시키는 꿈을 꾸고 있다.

한국의 새마을운동은 특별한 것이 아니다. 그저 "전국 3 만 3,267 개 마을에 시멘트 355 포대를 똑같이 나눠준 게 전부였다". (p.27, 정경민) 정부의 지원으로 마을을 부흥시킨 마을은 1 만 6600 개가 고작이었다. 나머지 마을들은 시멘트만 낭비하고 말았다. 그렇지만 다음해에 성과 있는 마을에만 시멘트 500 포와 철근 1 톤씩을 추가로 대줬다. 이런 정부의 선별지원은 마을간 경쟁을 촉발시키면서 각 마을들은 근면-자조-협동의 정신아래 뜻을 모아 마을을 부흥시켜 나갔다. 도로는 아스팔트로 새로 깔렸으며 초가집들은 더욱 효율성 있는 콘크리트건물로 바뀌었다. 이동수단이 늘고 효율이 높아지면서 자연스럽게 제조업과 중공업도 자리를 잡기 시작했다. 남수단의 대통령인 살바 키이르가 한국의 새마을운동에 관심을 보이고 있는 건 이 때문이다.

남수단과 대한민국 (다른 점)

　　남한과 남수단의 같은 점은 많지만 다른 점 또한 많다. 무엇보다 한국에선 기름이 나지 않는다. 현재 남수단에선 50 만 배럴의 원유가 생산되고 있다(Wall Street Journal, Monday, July 11, 2001 page A11, Connors and Fick). 오늘날 기름은 너무나 중요한 전략적 자원임과 동시에 엄청난 이득을 남겨준다. 남수단 재정수입의 97%를 차지하는 기름 수익은 50 년 전 아무것도 없었던 남한과 달리 다른 사업을 시작할 수 있는 초기 자금을 마련해줄 수 있다. 기름뿐 아니라　　　　　남수단엔　　　　　철광석, 금,　　　은, 구리, 알루미늄, 석탄, 우라늄, 크롬 시간, 아연, 운모, 다이아몬드, 석영, 텅스텐 등 많은 자연광물이 나오며, 4 천 100 만 에이커에 달하는 땅에서 농사가 가능하다. 남수단에서 나는 농산물에는　　　　　　　　"파인애플, 망고, 파파야의, 사탕수수, 면화, 사탕수수, 기장, 밀, 고구마, 카사바, 참깨 등이 있으며 더욱 많은 종류의 농작물을 키울 수 있는 여건이 갖춰져 있다." (South Sudan Birth of a Nation, published by government of South Sudan). 또한, 남 수단에 있는 보마(Boma) 사파리 월드 및 Sudd 의 습지와 남 수단 자연국립공원은 많은 수의 kob and topis (영양의 두 종류), 퍼팔로, 코끼리, 기린, hartebeests (또 다른 영양의 한 종류), and 사자. 를 보유하고 있다. 이 자연 자원을 이용하여 관광산업에 투자한다면 엄청난 이득을 창출할 수 있을 것이다

　　또한, 21 세기 아프리카의 첫 독립국이라는 사실이 가져다 주는 이점도 만만치 않다. 전세계에서 지원을 아끼지 않으며, 특히 UN 에서는 첫 아프리카 평화 종전 국 가 된 덕분에 미국, 영국, 중국, 독일, 프랑스, 이탈리아, 인도 등 많은 나라의 지원을 이끌어낼 수 있었다. 거의 아무것도 없이

성공을 이뤄낸 한국에 비하면 벌써 많은 이점을 갖고 시작하는 셈이다.

문제

남 수단엔 많은 장점이 있지만 많은 문제 또한 있다. 일단, 너무나 다양한 인종과 부족이 독립적으로 살아가고 있다. 토착민도 세 종족으로 나뉜다. Nilotic, Nilo-Hamitic 과 South0Western Sudanic 민들이 있는데, 그 중에서도 Nilotic 중에만 35 가지의 다른 부족이 다른 관습을 유지하며 살고 있다. 종교 또한 기독교, 전통 아프리카 종교와 이슬람이 대립하고 있어 더욱 난해한 문제를 만들고 있다. 남녀 지위도 불공평 하고, 무엇보다 군벌의 세력을 약화시키는 게 시급하다. 군벌들은 자신의 세력을 남, 북 수단에 흡수당하지 않으려고 약탈과 살인을 서슴지 않으며, 남, 북 수단과의 통합에 강력히 반대하고 있다.

지형적인 문제 또한 무시 할 수 없다. 남 단은 3 면이 바다인 남한과 달리 사방이 땅인 국가로, 바다를 통한 무역을 할 수가 없다. 특히나, 남수단에서 나는 많은 자원은 다른 나라를 통과하지 않고는 수출할 수가 없다. 남수단의 수입의 97%를 차지하는 기름이지만 모든 무역수단이 북수단에 있기 때문에 북수단은 남수단 석유 수입의 50%를 달라고 으름장을 놓고 있다. 현재 그 문제를 해결하기 위해 남수단의 남쪽에 있는 나라들을 통해 해상 무역을 꾀하고 있으나, 무거운 무역세금을 어떻게 해결해낼지는 의문이다.

북수단과의 타협 또한 아직 해결 해야 할 중요한 문제이다. 아비에이, 남코르도판, 블루나일지역 같은 분쟁지역은 남, 북 수단 전부 한치도 양보 할 수 없는 중요한 전략적 지점임과 동시에 비옥한 토지와 무엇보다

유전지대가 있다. 특히 아비에이는 남수단의 최고 부족인 딩가족의 발상지이기 때문에 남수단으로선 포기하기 어려운 곳이다.

이 밖에도 다양한 인종, 종교, 군벌세력, 무역로의 활성화, 북 수단과의 타협, 분쟁 지역의 타협, 등 많은 문제가 남아 있지만, 가장 시급한 문제 중 하나는 개인 생활의 발전이다. 남수단에는 은행 점포가 30 개밖에 안 되며, 산업시설들은 전쟁 중 파괴되거나 사용할 수 없게 됐다. 포장도로는 남수단 전체에서 50 킬로미터 밖에 되지 않으며, 통신수단과 미디어는 말 할 것도 없이 빈약하다. 남수단에는 25 개의 라디오 방송국이 있으나, 텔레비전은 두 개의 방송국밖에 없다. 어린이 중 30%는 학교를 다니지 않고 있으며 어른의 87.1%가 글을 읽을 줄 모른다. (Wikipedia)

교육

남 수단의 문제를 해결하려면 많은 것이 필요하다. 일단 돈이 필요하고 그 돈을 정부가 착복하지 않고 도로나 공업에 투자하여 많은 사람들이 안정적으로 살아갈 수 있게 하는 것이 중요하다. 안정적인 월급이 들어오고, 안정적인 집에서 안정적인 가정을 꾸려 걱정 없이 살수 있다면, 사회는 안정이 될 것이고, 국가는 부흥하게 될 것이다. 하지만, 그 부흥을 오래 지속시키려면 교육이 필수다. 남한의 예를 들자면 세계 교육비 1 위, 학생의 93%가 고등학교를 졸업하며, 교육에 관해서는 핀란드에 이어, 세계의 모범 국가다.

'한강의 기적'이 가능했던 것도 유별난 교육열 덕분이었다. 자연광물이나 자원, 땅의 소유권은 뺏길 수 있지만 사람은 빼앗을 수 없기 때문이다. 일본 제국주의는

강점기 시절 35 년 동안 한국의 모든 것을 빼앗아 갔지만 사람만은 약탈할 수 없었다. 일제 강점기 혹은 세계 2 차 대전 이후 66 년이 지나기까지, 남한의 교육열은 사람들의 희망이자 유일하게 수출할 수 있었던 아주 중요한 자원이 되었다. 전쟁의 여파로 아무것도 없는 남한에서는 "1962 년 10 월 상업차관으로 1 억 5,000 만 마르크를 5000 명의 광부와 2000 명의 간호사의 3 년 노동을 약속으로 빌려주었다" (p.17, 정경민)

가능성

앞서 지적했듯 남수단에는 아직 발견되지도 않은 많은 광물과 비옥한 농지가 널려있다. 전쟁의 여파가 끝나고 사람들이 희망을 갖고 평화적으로 일어선다면 남수단은 충분히 부흥할 가능성이 있다. 공업 단지와 산업시설이 활성화 되고, 주위 국가들의 협조아래 항구를 이용해 바다와 연결이 된다면, 아프리카의 선진국이 될 수도 있다.

바로 여기서 가능성이 생긴다. 남수단뿐만이 아니라 세계 많은 사람들에게 가능성이 열리는 것이다. 수단에 널려있는 자원을 캐내고, 가공할 수 있게 만드는 것은 바로 사람이기 때문에 투자 가능성은 무한정으로 열리게 되는 것이다. 광물, 농업, 산업, 통신, 및 여러 분야에서 투자의 무한한 가능성이 열리고, 또한, 남수단이 교육에 힘을 써 준다면, 아프리카의 모델이 될 수도 있다. 현재 많은 문제를 안고 있지만 하나씩 천천히 좋은 방향으로 풀어나간다면 아프리카뿐만 아니라 전 세계에서도 인정받는 국가가 될 수 있다.

Works Cited

"BBC NEWS | UK | Education | South Korea's Education Success." BBC News - Home. BBC News, 13 Sept. 2005. Web. 10 Oct. 2011. <http://news.bbc.co.uk/2/hi/uk_news/education/4240 668.stm>.

"Education in Sudan." Wikipedia, the Free Encyclopedia. Web. 10 Oct. 2011. <http://en.wikipedia.org/wiki/Education_in_Sudan>.

Fick, Maggie. "Work Begins for South Sudan." Wall Street Journal (2011/7/11): A11+. Print.

"Southern Sudan - Wildlife Conservation Society." WCS.org - Wildlife Conservation Society. Web. 11 Oct. 2011. <http://www.wcs.org/where-we-work/africa/southern-sudan.aspx>.

"Emperor Justinian and the Byzantine Empire"
James Park, Jr.

Rome was taken down in 410. The eastern emperor of Constantinople, Theodosius II, barely helped the western capital. Soon after, the ministers surrounded Constantinople with great walls. It was known as the Theodosian Wall. These walls were up until 1453 when opposing forces broke through. This wall helped the survival of the Roman Empire's Capital. With Theodosius II on the throne, Constantinople became "The Ruling City". The emperors went in the Great Palace and were let in by Bosphorus. When the emperor showed at the Hippodrome, the supporters or rivals would chant or criticize with rhythmic shouting. 'Greens' and 'Blues' reminded people that politics was no game.

Everyone in the city should have seen trails of smoking villages. Barbarians would raid villages and people would walk from the city walls. During the 5th and 6th century, Constantinople combined the city-state pride and high moral of an outpost with vast amounts of resources. However, at the inception of this time period, Constantinople was still avoiding the northern capital. The biggest gaps in society during the 4th century were not between the east and west but north and south.

Theodosius II was raised in a family of Latin generals. In 438, the Latin compilations of Imperial laws were known as the "Theodosian Code". As long as the court and military were connected, the current language would be Latin. Latin had always been the formal language they used in court. Eastern Roman schools would also teach Latin.

But Constantinople stopped focusing on Rome but on Greece. Greeks who didn't learn Latin would help 'Old Rome' in the west during the 4th and 5th century. But those who did know Latin would travel to 'New Rome' to help out Constantinople. Latin survived as their main language in Constantinople.

Strangely during the 5th century, Latins themselves were decreasing in population. From the 3rd century onwards, the Roman army was slowly decreasing. By the end of the 5th century, the Roman army was nearly completely gone.

Anastasius whose reign lasted from 491 to 518 and Justinian whose reign lasted for 527 to 565 were considered the two greatest emperors. Anastasius was a palace official until his late middle ages. Justinian was a nephew of a Latin soldier from the Balkans who was known as Justin.

From the 5th century, Rome's new identity was as a part of the Constantinople Empire. The architects of the Greek towns were close to unknown. John of Lydia was one who made one thousand gold pieces in one year. Not only was he an architect but he also a learned Latin, a poet, and an author. Agitation was against unnecessary taxes.

In 399, a future bishop, Synesius of Cyrene thought of a policy excluding the barbarians and added that to his speech. Procopius wrote his *Secret History* in 550 that summarized "Black Book" of the reign of Justinian. They all learned from Thucydides a tradition of writing once in a while. Procopius died in 562 as a secretary to Justinian's famous general Belisarius.

The nomad empire of Attila has risen from 434 to 453 whose power controlled the plains of Hungary to Holland and the Caucasus. It marked the turning-point in Roman history. The first emergence in the northern world of the barbarian empire was equal to Rome. The 4th century Roman Empire had still thought of themselves as a civilized world and embraced it.

The Sassanian Empire was the only other organized empire they knew. During the 5th century, the myth of the 'middle kingdom' was overwhelming. The Eastern Romans came to learn that their empire was only one state amongst many others. During the mid-5th century, Olympiodorus of Thebes in Egypt was the first colorful representative of a long and rich tradition of Byzantine diplomats. He went on missions as far as Rome to Nubia and the Dnieper who was entertained by a parrot who fluently spoke pure Attic Greek.

The emperors suggested that diplomacy should be an important piece of warfare. Exactly at the same time, the western senators of Constantinople were made to sell their wives' jewelry to pay for the subsidies that brought down the empire of Attila. Marinus the Syrian was a praetorian prefect of Anastasius, who saved the eastern empire when the western half collapsed. He would leave a pen and ink right beside his bedside and a lamp. He would wright down all of his thoughts on a roll and tells them to the emperor during the daytime. It advised him how to act. Constantinople had become the goal of ambitious provincials far from the center of the Greek empire from which the bureaucracy was recruited.

At the end of the 5th century, Daniel the young Syrian from Mesopotamia was on his way to practice asceticism in Jerusalem. He was warned in a vision to go to Constantinople instead. The 'Ruling City' had evolved into the 'Holy City'. But the history of Constantinople in the late 5th century was known for their gifted immigrants. But the talents along the classical world were not enough that the empire of Constantinople should become Greek.

The Patriarchs Theophilus and Cryil of Egypt were leading the Greek world. Under Anastasius reign, Syrian merchants were trading to as far as center of Asia and Gaul. Syrians were also the ones who filled the Greek world with music.

The Council of Chalcedon in 451 was held by the emperor of Marcian and took advantage of Greek opinions. When the settlement arrived at Chalcedon, the eastern Christians were extremely upset. For the next 200 years, emperors faced the difficult quest to restore the balance.

On April 9, 491, Emperor Zeno died in Constantinople freeing a part of what was controlled by the Goths. They failed to get rid of the heresy. "In 482 Zeno and Patriarch Acacius together had sought to paper over the differences by affirming that Christ was both God and man, avoiding the word 'nature' altogether; but had only aroused the hostility of both sides." (John Julius Norwich, p. 57) In 484, Pope Felix III was furious with the Patriarchate of Constantinople and banned him from the church. The Patriarch of Constantinople then instantly reacted back and excommunicated the Pope back.

In the new Patriarchate of Constantinople, Justin was a poor peasant and married to a slave. However, his nephew was the prodigy that gave him the advantage. The nephew was smart and invented his uncle's elevation. In 482, Justinian was born. His uncle raised Justinian to receive great education, and he was an officer at Schole at the time of Anastasius's death. "Justinian immediately showed himself willing to be guided by him in all things, and for the rest of his life thereafter was content to be his puppet." (John Julius Norwich, p.60)"To Justinian, then, belongs the credit for the most important achievement of his uncle's reign: the healing of the breach with Rome, which had begun with the pinning of the sentence of excommunication on to the robes of Patriarch Acacius in 484." (John Julius Norwich, p. 60)

On March 25, 519, the Pope's messenger arrived in Constantinople, and met Justinian. On March 27, 519, Patriarch John declared that the old and new church combine to become one at Saint Sophia.

Justinian met Theodora around a year or two later. "Theodora was not an ideal match. Her father had been a bear-keeper at the Hippodrome, and her mother an acrobat - antecedents which was more than enough to debar her from polite society." (John Julius Norwich, p.61) "Before long she had graduated to being Constantinople's most notorious courtesan. She was certainly a changed woman when she returned to Constantinople." (John Julius Norwich p.61-62) "Justinian too favoured the Blues, and it was probably through them that he first met Theodora, by now in her middle thirties. He was at once captivated, and determined to make her his wife." (John Julius Norwich, p.63) On April 4th 527, they were married and became co-emperor and empress. Theodora helped Justinian with his decisions and gave him all the benefits.

During Justinian's rule, there was much unrest, because of Barbarian invasions, particularly in Italy. Witigis wrote to Justinian to point out that the murder of Amalasuntha was their reason for the invasion of Italy. The regards were canceled through the death of Theodahad. Witigis asked Catholic Bishops of Italy to make prayers for peace. Theodahad had also preferred peace over war. It reminded Witigis that the quick and correct way to peace was a simple surrender.

Early in the year, the Gothic levy was summoned along with around 20,000 troops. By February, this advance was taking place. Belisarius was the Roman leader, and he flung to the northwest to hold off Perugia, Spoletium, and Narnia. During their first engagement, the Goths showed their brutal strengths. However, in dose combat, Goths lost 1,000 men and were forced to retreat.

Once the Goths were reinforced, they soon returned to the fight. After that conflict, not a single person was recognized because all the dust on their faces. Belisarius was locked out and most people thought he died in battle.

Once Belisarius was recognized and allowed in by the guards, he was preparing battle strategies. An emissary of the barbarian King Wacis arrived at the Salarian Gate to summon the city to surrender. After denouncing Romans for abandoning the Gothic government, Belisarius returned to arrange for the next day's defence. Spending all night planning and getting little to no sleep, he was very optimistic, yet no one was certain why he was.

Witigis was scarce in the number of troops needed to besiege Rome. He constructed seven camps outside the city surrounding them. However, this blockade was not complete. The first step to take in place was to cut off the aqueducts, one of Rome's greatest inventions. The aqueducts was basically a bridge-like passage way of transportation of water from the mountains to the city. Even after blocking off Rome's water supply, the barbarians were not able to create that big of a crisis. However, it affected the everyday activities possible, such as public bathes.

But not long after, the loss of not having watermills was an urgent matter. Belisarius set up two boats holding together what somewhat resembled a watermill. The watermills were powering a machine which grinded all the corn that needed grinding. Belisarius was doing well and out-smarting his opponents with is emergency responses.

Wittigis's spokesman spoke like a patron describing the hardship and misery through the siege upon Romans. Belisarius's answer scared his own people. He answered with a complete confident no. When his offer was rejected, Witigis planned another assault to capture the city.

On the 18th day, the sun was rising and the Goths were in seven columns. They were marching toward the Praenestine Gate and the Vatican. As they were beginning their assault, excited Romans were yelling criticism at the opposing commanders. They still continued to advance.

Belisarius finally stepped into action with a bow aiming for a commander who was leading the operation. With two shots, he confirmed their commander's death. The Romans had two major advantages. First, they had geographic advantage because of the height of their wall and their knowledge about the nearby lands. Their second major advantage was having massive range support, which not only included archers but artillery. Archers were shooting down at the Goths yet they couldn't do anything about it.

The Goths were in range of the Romans and began their assault. As Roman troops were engaged in the battle, archers were massacring from above. As it was nearly twilight, the destruction caused by the Goths expected to do lead to the Fall of Rome. However, the Goths suffered a major loss of 30,000 men. Besides the damage done to their army and equipment, the Goths finally realized that this war would be difficult to win. This contrasted with their stereotype of the Romans. "Their pride would not permit them to look upon the Roman army as anything but riff-raft:" (G.P. Baker, p.155)

After the battle, Belisarius realized himself as one of the best strategic leaders. He also knew he could improve through this war. "Like a wise man, Belisarius was much more interested in his weaknesses than his strengths." (G.P. Baker, p.155)

Belisarius told Justinian that if they were to continue to fight this war, they would not only lose their army but they would completely lose Italy. Rome being a city far inland, they weren't expected to live their lives happily without food and reinforcement was difficult.

All the pressures of the Barbarians took a toll on Justinian's heath. Although Justinian's health recovered, the empire around him was crumbling to his feet. Not only was Byzantine suffering but Persia as well. Choroes, and Persian general raided the Byzantine territory, but this backfired on them.

During that time in Byzantine, there was a raging plague which was brought back to Persia. This plague killed 25% of their population. Rome in general wasn't doing too well, especially in the absence of Belisarius. Totila was the Goth's king, and he darted straight around the helpless Byzantines. Totila was there to end the war that has been active for decades.

Under a year, Totila destroyed most of Belisaurius's work. The generals of Byzantine wrote to Justinian that they couldn't continue defending Rome. Justinian once again called for Belisarius, while in an argument with Theodora. Belisarius managed to defend the center of Italy. However, everyday had a new fresh disaster. Belisaurius was told to protect Rome against the Goths with so few troops. Belisaurius sent a messenger back to the palace requesting for veterans.

Instead of following though with his missions, he spent time in the capital and got married. Soon after, he notified Justinian. Even after the request was requested, they couldn't finance new troops. Justinian sent a small handful of units. The army ultimately was made of depressed soldiers. Belisarius was desperate enough to send his wife in 548.

When his wife, Antonina got to the palace, she saw Justinian in grief and Theodora dead. In 549, Justinian once again called for Belisarius and greeted him like a brother. In Belisarius's honor, Justinian built a bronze statue.

As Rome was being besieged by Totila, Belisaurius was hiding. Justinian just then realized he would need one good general in order to save Rome. Narses was a veteran already in his seventies, like Justinian. Evens with his old age and strange experience, Justinian thought he was making the correct decision. Narses was equipped with supplies that were denied to other generals. With nearly ten times the men Belisarius had, Narses was prepared with troops and money.

Once again, someone else was there to take Belisarius's credit. Romans were also beginning to revolt against the barbarian king. The brilliant leader in control was Athanagild. In Spain, the rebels had taken Cordoba and were asking for help to take over Seville. Due to all the resources they were spending in the war to save Italy, Byzantine was nearly bankrupt. Spain was also in a desperate situation, and Justinian couldn't refuse to deny the opportunity. When Justinian chose Liverius to be the new general, they were in complete shock. Liverius was ninety years old. But he was an excellent choice by Justinian, especially with decades more of experience. Leading an army of few hundred men, he was prepared to save Spain.

Narses was prepared to save Italy right until the plague affected their time table. Along with the plague was an earthquake damaging the Hagia Sophia. With Byzantine fighting three wars, it took Justinian five years to repair and six to build. Justinian reduced the military power and decided to bribe the enemies to leave them.

When Justinian was first placed on the throne, he had around 500,000 soldiers. After the disaster including the plague, it was close to 150,000 soldiers. In 559, a group of Huns intruded into the city, yet nothing could be done since all of his army was at war. This is when Belisarius's last task for Justinian began. With years of experience, he ambushed the Huns, extremely weakening them. He even managed to throw them out of the walls of Constantinople with retired troops and volunteers.

Justinian dismissed Belisarius because of his lack of trust for the leaders. He decided to finish this on his own. Once again, Belisarius's credit was taken. After bribing the Huns to leave, he celebrated for achieving peace. Narses did an outstanding job in Italy protecting Rome. Even though Belisarius was well aware he deserved more attention, he was loyal and received his humiliation in silence.

Belisarius died and only eight months later on November 14, 565, Justinian died. Justinian, Belisarius, and Procopius, who was the historian at the time, were known as the three Byzantine giants. When they all died in 565, it was known as the deaths of all three Byzantine giants.

In Justinian's 83 years on the throne, he well improved Byzantine. He greatly improved the economy and the judicial system. He controlled the Mediterranean sea, once Roman again. The golden domes of Hagia Sophia still stand. It was one of the most powerful visions during his ruling.

Emperor Justinian is particularly wee-known for his achievement in law. This is a description of the significance of Justinian's law achievements during the Middle Ages.

Law was a general benefactor protecting lives and would punish the ones doing wrong. "The application of written law was fundamental to Byzantium thoughtout its long history," (Judith Herrin, p.70) It secured ordinary citizens by protecting their inheritance, property, and family problems. Byzantine law was based off the Roman legal system.

Rome's legal system contributed to the worlds civilization between 500 B.C. and 100 A.D. In 429, the emperor ordered legal experts to gather all the books about Roman legal structure. It was then published into a single volume. The Codex Theodosianus was shown to Constantinople in November of 437. Copies of the volume were sent to Old Rome.

During 313 and 437, all laws involving Christianity were removed. "Contradictions and confusions between different laws had been removed and a simplified system was established." (Judith Herrin, p.71) This was applied in both halves of the empire, and they were focusing on this in the East. The Roman colony of Berytus's fame was growing until the earthquake in 550 or 551.

Severus was a Monophysite Patriarch of Antioch and studied in law, during 512-518. Around a century after the publication of the Codex Theodosianus, Justinian assumed imperial power. In 528, he set up a meeting of then experienced lawyers commanded by Tribonian. He was the chief legal official; he would send it through all the imperial constitutions to impose orders and adapt provisions. This all occurred during the sixth century. When this was completed in 529, they issued copies of the Codex Constitution. The simplified collection did not survive. However, it was summarized in the Corpus Iuns Civilis.

The second stage of reform occurred during 530-534, and Justinian appointed sixteen lawyers to fix the contradicting laws people have noticed throughout the years. In 533, an outline of the Roman laws was designed to guide students, who were published in the Institutes. Justinian issued many more laws which were called the new laws. It was named to tell apart from the old and the new laws.

During this time period, Justinian's was considered one of the most outstanding legal systems and was not changed until the fall of Byzantium during the 1400's. The knowledge of the Corpus Iuris Civilis was nearly instinct between seventh century to the late eleventh century. The original copy was estimated to have been made during the sixth century and had been hidden in southern Italy.

By the middle of the twelfth century, Gratian's collection of canon law, also known as the Decretum, was worked on during 1130-1140. In 1158, Emperor Fredrick I Barbarossa encouraged his students into expanding their knowledge of the ancient sources of both laws. "Roman law is characterized by its attention to the law of persons," (Judith Herrin, p.73).

That was the beginning of the fair trial, when one was treated equally, whether one was enslaved or free. By the sixth century, a quickly growing community of church-related regulations existed. They were made in both Antioch and Constantinople around 580. The Nomokannon in Fourteen Titles were most likely assembled in territories of Herakleios during 610-641. A similar process was already in place when Pope Hormisdas, during 514-523, commissioned Latin translations of the glorious Greek canons. The canons of the oecurnenical and others were from 38 papal letters, dated around 384 to 498, which were known as the decretals.

When the Easterns included the rules of St. Basil and laws of Justinian, Dionysius included papal ruling which raised the level of how strict everyone must be to follow the rule. Besides, the twelfth book of law gave prominence to issue of Christian faith. During the sixth century, only some of Justinian's subsequent Novals extended to the Christians morality.

Civil and ecclesiastical laws worked together in the Christian Empire of Byzantine. After the disaster of an earthquake in Bergtus in 550 or 551, Alexandria became the most popular legal and philosophical training outside of Byzantine. They taught a Christianized version of Aristotelian philosophy. After Alexandria being overthrown by the Arabs in the seventh century, all the legal and philosophical education was in Byzantium.

Using Institutes as a basis of legal education caused students to finish the study of law in five years. However, there were only two professional groups of lawyers. There were advocates and the notaries. Before the sixth century, Latin people studied Roman laws, but they were now replaced by Greek laws. It was call The Courpus Iuris Civilis, which came out in November 534 and was soon translated, but all of Justinian's subsequent new laws came out in Greek only.

During the late thirteenth century, close to no Latin was spoken in Byzantium. The emperors continued to make laws based on the influences Christianity made. For example, the Ekloga of 740 is a short law code of Leo III, which also replaced physical mutilation with capital punishment. In the late ninth century, the Baskilika was a six-volume edition of the imperial law. There were sixty books arranged by subject and in chronological order.

In 882-883, Patriarch Photios wrote and translated the second edition of the Nomokanon. The second edition ultimately helped the newly built Bulgarian Church. Until 1204, there was a revival of interest in both civil and ecclesiastical law. The third prologue to the Nomokanon was writing by a canon lawyer by the name of Theodore Bestes in 1089-1090. Under Theophilos, reign between 829-842, an imperial ceremony of riding from the Great Palace to the church of Balchernai and back to the Great Palace on Friday started. It provided opportunities for ordinary citizens to appeal to the emperor.

It can be seen that it was Emperor Justinian, who fell in love with and married an actress, who started the aggressive process of reforming laws that led to a type of democratization of laws.

Bibliography

Baker, G.P. *Justinian: The Last Roman Emperor*. New York: Cooper Square Press, 2002.

Brown, Peter. *The World of Late Antiquity*, New York: W.W. Norton & Company Inc., 1989.

Brownworth, Lars. *Lost to The West: The Forgotten Byzantine Empire That Rescued Western Civilization*. Random House: New York, 2009.

Herrin, Judith. *Byzantium: The Surprising Life of a Medieval Empire*. Princeton: Princeton University, 2007.

Norwich, John Julius. *A Short History of Byzantium*. New York: Vintage books, 1997.

"Visual Evoked Potential
and the Neuroanatomical Connection"

Ariel Raimundo Choi

Room 604N is the modest, yet special, workplace of Dr. James Gordon, professor of psychology and world-renowned neurophysiologist. Located on the 6th floor of Hunter College of the City of New York, this room has been the site of numerous research ventures on the part of Dr. Gordon and his associates. Dr. Gordon's first publication dates all the way back to 1988, when his work appeared in the Color Research and Application publication. In 2006, he published his studies of visual evoked potential under the title of "Luminance Contrast Mechanisms in Humans: Visual Evoked Potentials and a Nonlinear Model." With this publication, Dr. Gordon and his research group adopted the notion of VEP (visual evoked potential) as the heart of their research. I can attest to this fact, as I myself participated in Dr. Gordon's research group during the summer of 2011. Every week of the summer, I commuted to Hunter College and witnessed, first-hand, the work of Dr. Gordon.

Evidently, I did not work only with Dr. Gordon. Often times, Dr. Vance Zemon (professor of psychology at Ferkauk Graduate School of Psychology and prominent neurophysiologist himself) would come to the lab and provide us with some valuable assistance. I was first introduced to Dr. Zemon by Dr. Dongsoo Kim (the father of a schoolmate of mine), who had worked with Dr. Zemon in the past. (In fact, I had my first contact with Dr. Zemon before I met anybody else in the lab, including Dr. Gordon). One of Dr. Zemon's students, a graduate student by the name of Paige M. Weinger, was responsible for monitoring and directing my research over the summer. She has been researching under the guidance of Dr. Gordon and Dr. Zemon for several years, and has attained a strong understanding of VEP. Adeola Hardwood, Theresa Navalta, Sarvin Azizgolshani, Jean-Phillippe Michel, Valerie Nunez, and Janet Izrailova — all students at Hunter College — were also my colleagues this past summer at the Gordon Lab.

Room 604N is, in actuality, composed of three smaller rooms: Dr. Gordon's office, the organizational room, and the research room. As one passes through the green door indicating the entrance to 604N, one is immediately introduced to the organizational room, which has dimensions of approximately 8 ft by 20ft. There are three narrow tables arranged along the right wall and five feet from each other. The table closest to the entrance serves no specific purpose, but the other two support their respective desktop computers. These computers, though not directly incorporated into the research, serve as databases crucial to the success of the Gordon Lab; if they were to irreparably malfunction, all the data acquired over the years would vanish.

As one then turns to the left, one immediately sees the door to Dr. Gordon's personal office. The office, a long, narrow compartment of space, is occupied predominantly by metal drawer chests filled with old research papers. Next, the research room can be reached (upon entering 604N) by walking all the way across the main (organizational) room and turning to the right. This room, by far the largest of the three, has only a few distinctive features: two large sinks along the opposite end of the room, in addition to three booth-like structures along another side of the room. These small booth-like structures aligned were the specific sites of our research. Each holds the essentials of a VEP test, namely an EEG adapter and computer.

EEG, short for electroencephalography, is the recording of electrical activity in the brain, chiefly the cerebral cortex (Robson et. al., 2003, p.130). This proves to be a useful tool for neuroscientists, as "electrophysiological techniques (electroencephalogram (EEG); evoked potentials (EPs)) provide functional evaluation of the nervous system" (Guérit, 2005, p.415). There lies a distinct relationship between EPs and EEGs: "EPs correspond to the EEG modifications induced by sensory stimuli or cognitive activities" (Guérit, 2005, p.416). It should be noted, however, that EP waveforms, in general, exhibit lower amplitudes. This renders brain stem analysis possible (although the extensive use of averaging techniques is required), in contrast to general EEGs, which focus predominantly on the cerebral cortex.

EPs can be classified in three different ways: visual, auditory, and somatosensory. Visual evoked potential (VEP) is essentially a measure that revolves around Isaac Newton's fundamental notion that "pictures, propagated by motion along the fibers of the optic nerves in the brain, are the cause of vision." Since their onset, VEP recordings have been frequently utilized by neurologists to diagnose neurological conditions like Alzheimer's and Multiple Sclerosis (Regragui-Aafif, 1990, p.1). A VEP test serves as an ideal diagnosis tool due to its non-invasiveness (it does not require penetration of skin) and relative simplicity.

An EP is characterized by "a succession of peaks, which are characterized by their latencies and amplitudes; each peak reflects the activation of one sensory relay or a limited network of sensory structures. Short-latency EPs evaluate the brain-stem, the subcortical somatosensory pathways, and the primary parietal cortex (N20). Middle-latency EPs provide assessment of the temporal (middle-latency auditory evoked potentials (AEPs)), parietal and frontal (middle-latency Somatosensory evoked potentials (SEPs), and the occipital (Visual evoked potentials (VEPs)) cortex. Long latency exogenous and cognitive EPs depend on multiple cortical generators" (Guérit, 2005, p 416). Thus, in the context of my research at the Gordon lab, I studied middle-latency EPs.

Fundamentally, VEP test indicate the "integrity of the visual pathways and have been used extensively to monitor the activity of post-receptoral chromatic mechanisms" (Robson et. al., 2003, p.130). Thus, researchers are likely to use this tool to investigate how the visual pathways react both during, and after, the stimulus is presented to the research participant. (One particular method of stimulus display is addressed in the following paragraph.) VEP functions under the principle that "every contrast reversal is followed by evoked activity in the visual cortex" (Skrandies, 2003, p.79). After all, one of the key functions of the visual system is the perception of luminance contrast; "parallel neural pathways [are] dedicated to the processing of positive and negative contrast information" (García-Quispe, Gordon, Zemon, 2009). Thus, a commonly used stimulus is a "moving" checkerboard, in which the component squares reverse in contrast (i.e. black squares become to white squares, and vice versa, after some specified time interval). More technically put, "horizontal square-wave gratings contrast reversed" at a frequency of roughly 7.5 Hz (García-Quispe, Gordon, Zemon, 2009). Another commonly used stimulus pattern in the Gordon Lab is the windmill pattern. Though rather rudimentary, such patterns are particularly effective in illustrating general developments in the visual pathways. Specifically, at least in the context of the Gordon Lab, the VEP serves as a tool used "to investigate the developmental change in the contrast response function and the neural mechanisms that contribute to this change" (García-Quispe, Gordon, Zemon, 2009).

Another fundamental notion in VEP testing is the principle that "different frequencies yield brain responses of different strengths" (Skrandies, 2003, p.79). This is to be expected, as one would logically deduce that stronger stimuli yield stronger visual responses. The amplitudes of the VEP waveforms, which are representative of the strength of the response, are also largest when the stimulus is changing at a rate of 6 reversals per second. This is generally the peak rate, in terms of the resulting amplitude; once the stimulus is reversing at a pace that exceeds 6 reversals/second, the response diminishes in power.

All of these computers in the research room are equipped with the program Neucodia v. 3.5, created by Verisci™. The Verisci™ internet page describes the Neucodia system as a "novel electroencephalographic (EEG) device that provides select stimuli, synchronized data acquisition, amplification with adjustable filter settings, rich data processing tools in time and frequency domains, and statistical analyses." Neucodia is relatively user-friendly, as its mouse-controlled graphical interface facilitates and expedites VEP measurements. It is also equipped with a stimulus generator that produces the visual stimuli shown in the VEP tests. What renders Neucodia unique, however, is its efficient data processing/displaying system ; data can be rapidly processed and displayed in a variety of ways. A sine-cosine plot, which depicts the Frequency Components of Interest (FCI), is one of them. Data can also be analyzed in amplitude/phase plots, which incorporate sweep variables such as luminance contrast as the independent x-axis variables.

Using the Neucodia system, we measured the VEPs of an eclectic (in terms of age and general mental health) pool of research participants. In a typical three-hour meeting, one or two tests were run in a dark, ideally noiseless, room. To perform this test, a participant is first seated about 5 feet from a CRT (cathode ray tube) monitor at eye-level. (It should be noted that two vision tests – one at five feet away and the other at twenty – would have to be conducted prior to the VEP exam, so as to consider the participant's vision during data analysis). Three gold-cup electrodes are subsequently attached on the participant's scalp. The distance between the occipital bone and the midpoint of the space between the eyebrows is then measured. Furthermore, the Internation 10-20 system is followed: "standard gold-cup electrodes [are] attached to these midline sites. One electrode at Oz (positive lead; located at 10% of the distance from the inion to the nasion) [is] referenced to another one at Cz (negative lead; at 50% of the distance from the inion to the nasion) with a floating ground electrode placed at Pz (at 30% of this distance)" (García-Quispe, Gordon, Zemon, 2009). This measurement is crucial, as it determines the exact placements of the three electrodes (which can be marked, for convenience). Inaccurate electrode positions – and likewise, inaccurate tape-measurements –result in an "unclean" signal, as the VEP waveform will effectively be skewed. Before attaching these electrodes, however, skin preparation gel is applied on the three marked areas. Moreover, water-soluble paste (often used in electrical neurophysiological testing) is applied on the regions of the electrodes that will be in contact with the skin.

After the electrodes are firmly and correctly glued onto the scalp of the participant, the Neucodia system installed on the computer is launched. The system's stimulus generator then displays a series of visual patterns (evidently, one is under the premise that these patterns are already selected by the researcher by the time of testing) of varying frequencies (both spatial and chronometric), light-dark contrasts, etc.

My research group at the Gordon Lab used nine (though sometimes ten) test patterns. Two of these patterns were longer, and lasted 60 seconds, whereas the others were shorter, roughly five seconds each. A short condition would be run ten times, in straight succession, before the researcher moved on to the next pattern. To phrase it differently, a series of "steady-state sweeps" were run. In contrast, a longer pattern would be run only once. On a relevant note, the VEP test can be characterized as either binocular or monocular (evidently, depending on which eye(s) is (are) receiving the visual stimuli). In the end, the VEP session will have lasted roughly an hour.

It should be noted that the focus of a participant must be closely monitored during these longer patterns, as the loss of focus can disrupt the extraction of clean VEP waveforms that are reflective of the stimulus of visual pathways. It is not surprising that "factors such as the attention, motivation, or expectancy as well as the occurrence probability of stimuli determine the pattern of electrical brain activity" (Skrandies, 2003, p.80). Although this correlation is readily recognized throughout the neurophysiological research world, the extent to which focus and electrical brain activity are interrelated is not clearly defined. This broaches the logical question: "Can VEP be used to elucidate the strength of this relationship?" Indeed, it appears that an intensive VEP investigation, designed within the proper parameters, could succeed in providing a very specific answer to this issue, as "attention affects early steps of visual processing. Thus, the influence of attention and cognitive parameters on activation of the visual cortex can be studied electrophysiologically by recordings of VEP activity" (Skrandies, 2003, p.79).

Other external elements that could hinder the extraction of acceptable VEP data are disruptive sound, excessive luminance, or even the presence of impurities in the participant's scalp. While the effect of outside noises on the experiment can be diminished, somewhat, during data analysis (a certain frequency can be removed from the resulting graph by using Wiener filtering, for instance), unwanted sounds should be unconditionally avoided during experimentation. An unwanted light source can also skew the results, as excessive light will not only lower the participant's concentration, but also complicate the participant's vision process while the visual patterns are running. Oils and particles in the participant's skin can also impede the acquiring of clean data, as the electrodes will be unable to efficiently conduct the electrical activity in the brain. Lessening the impact of such potentially problematic elements will increase the chance of a successful VEP test.

Once the results are obtained, there are several methods that the experimenter can implement to extract VEP waveforms. As aforementioned, one can make use of "signal averaging which rejects the part of the electrical brain activity not related to external excitation" (Regragui-Aafif, 1990, p.20). This will render it possible to remove background noises that may have imposed an unwanted contribution to the experiment. A similar method of doing so is through adaptive filtering, which "utilizes two input signals x(n) and y(n) referred to as the primary signal and the reference signal" (Regragui-Aafif, 1990, p.25). The use of ADF requires significant mathematical analysis (complex algorithms are key to these analyses), as do many other VEP extraction methods. Moreover, ADF is preferred over the customary signal averaging method in cases of VEP extraction with only a few stimuli.

In order to achieve enhanced spectral resolution, the method of "windowing" can be incorporated into data handling. Windowing, which is done prior to data analysis, is essentially the truncation of data. The point of truncation is dependent on the location of the P100, which is a specific peak on the VEP waveform. My research group at Hunter College occasionally utilized the windowing tool, which rendered a closer analysis of the data both possible and convenient.

One of the most important tools that my research group utilized was that of "Fourier analysis." Fourier analysis is fundamentally designed to "derive amplitude and phase of the dominant (second harmonic) frequency in the response" (García-Quispe, Gordon, Zemon, 2009). In the context of Dr. Gordon's (and Dr. Zemon's) 2009 study with Dr. Leticia A. García-Quispe of the Center for Neural Science in New York University, Fourier analysis was used to "derive the amplitudes and phases of frequency components that occur at multiples of the stimulus frequency" (García-Quispe, Gordon, Zemon, 2009). These were then plotted against contrast. By so doing, Dr. Gordon and Dr. Zemon investigated how the contrast response

114

functions of the visual system change over the course of one's lifetime. (VEP testing was done on two groups: infants and adults.) What they discovered that the fitted contrast response functions of adults generally exhibited non-linear properties. Meanwhile, those of children were comparatively linear. The distinction is caused by the element of "shunting inhibition," which is another topic of itself. Essentially, shunting inhibition is the premise that the amplitudes of postsynaptic potentials, which are produced after the activation of the shunting inhibition synapse, incrementally decrease.

According to the aforementioned study," the net extracellular current flow generated by a large number of neurons primarily in the superficial layers of visual cortex. The most numerous cells in the neocortex are the pyramidal neurons in layers 2/3, and apical dendrites of pyramidal neurons are the main neuronal structures in the superficial layers of cortex" (García-Quispe, Gordon, Zemon, 2009). Dendrites are, on their basest level, "relatively short processes...which receive most inputs to the cell" (Blumenfeld, 2010, p.17). The term "apical" merely implies that these dendrites are located on the apex of a pyramidal cell. Pyramidal cells, it should be noted, are the "principal neurons of the hippocampus and subiculum" (Blumenfeld, 2010, p.831). The hippocampus and subiculum (Latin for "support") are two of the three parts of the hippocampal formation. This formation, which plays an invaluable role in cognitive and visual processing, is a structure of the brain's medial temporal lobe.

Meanwhile, the neocortex (the largest part of the brain) is the center of most visual processing. It contains four layers: the parieto-occipital fissure, Stria of Gennari, Calcarine fissure, and Optic tract. Three parallel channels of information function with another in this visual cortex; these three channels analyze motion, form , and color. "The magnocellular layers conveying information about movement and gross spatial features, project mainly to 4Cα. The parvocellular layers of the LGN, carrying fine spatial information, terminate mainly in layer 4Cβ. Information about color is also relayed by the parvocellular layers, as well as by the interlaminar zones, to specialized regions of cortical layers 2 and 3" (Blumenfeld, 2010, p.468). All of these structures work in conjunction, as well as with other structures (not mentioned here) that play a key role in spatial, form, and color analysis. These specific structures, however, are "in the middle of things" during higher-order visual processing.

One can even delve deeper into the system, and scrutinize the two major pathways involved in visual processing. Blumenfeld (2010) distinguishes the two in a succinct, clear manner (p.468). The dorsal pathways essentially respond to the question "Where?" (in other words, spatial distinction) and pertain to the parieto-occipital association cortex, a sublevel of the ponderous visual cortex. On the other hand, the ventral pathways respond to the question "What?" (in other words, form and color distinction) and pertain to the occipitotemporal association cortex (Blumenfeld, 2010, p.468).

This investigation into neuroanatomy can be pursued further into the molecular level. The amino acid GABA (gamma-aminobutyric acid) is an "inhibitory transmitter [that] reduces the likelihood of an action potential being generated in the postsynaptic cell" (LeDoux, 2002, p.53). In this way, it has regulatory functions. In conjunction with the transmitter, glutamate, GABA also plays the largest role in neurotransmission. These transmitters' binding to receptors in the brain is what induces "excitation and inhibition" (LeDoux, 2002, p.54). An excess amount of GABA has been related to mental illnesses like schizophrenia (a correlation that has prompted Dr. Gordon and Dr. Zemon to thoroughly understand the role of this amino acid).

Needless to say, all of the aforementioned structures (especially the pathways) are intensely tested during VEP examinations. The effect of GABA on normal visual processing, in fact, can be readily analyzed through VEP study. In reality, virtually an infinite number of neuroanatomical connections are prevalent during the processing of VEP stimulus patterns.

Over the years, "studies of the visual system have attracted many researchers...with attempts to understand its complex mechanism" (Regraui-Aafif, 1990, p.55). Indeed, there are many discoveries (about the visual system) left to make through neurophysiological experiments, and even these experiments have their frequent spatiotemporal limitations. Undoubtedly, there is a cornucopia of challenges that I will encounter in the future, as an active researcher, physician, and leading contributor to the growing field of neuroscience.

Bibliography

Blumenfeld, H. (2010). *Neuroanatomy through clinical cases* (2nd ed.). Sunderland: Sinauer Associates.

García-Quispe, L., Gordon, J., & Zemon, V. (2009) "Development of contrast mechanisms in humans: A VEP study." *Optometry and Vision Science*, 86, 708-716.

Guérit, J. M. (2005). "Evoked potentials in severe brain injury." In S. Laureys (Ed.), *The Boundaries of Consciousness: Neurobiology and Neuropathology* (pp. 415-426). The Netherlands: Elsevier.

LeDoux, J. (2002) *Synaptic Self: How Our Brains Become Who We Are*. New York: Viking Adult.

Regragui-Aafif, F. (1990). *Extraction and linear prediction modeling of the visual evoked potential*. New Brunswick: Rutgers, the State University of New Jersey.

Robson et. al. (2003). "Integration Times Reveal Mechanisms Responding to Insoluminant Chromatic Gratings: A Two-Centre Visual Evoked Potential Study." In J.D. Mollon, J. Pokomy, K. Knoblauch (Eds.) *Normal and defective colour vision* (pp. 130-137). London: Oxford University Press.

Skrandies, W. (2003). "Evoked Potentials Studies of Visual Information Processing." In A. Zani & A. M. Proverbio

(Ed.), *The Cognitive Electrophysiology of Mind and Brain* (pp. 71-92). Toronto: Academic Press.

www.ingramcontent.com/pod-product-compliance
Lightning Source LLC
Chambersburg PA
CBHW020005290326
41935CB00007B/310